HOOLIGANS, DOORMEN,
and the
TEN-METRE WALK

ELVIS WEBLEY

BALBOA.PRESS
A DIVISION OF HAY HOUSE

Balboa Press books may be ordered through booksellers or by contacting:

Balboa Press
A Division of Hay House
1663 Liberty Drive
Bloomington, IN 47403
www.balboapress.com
844-682-1282

Because of the dynamic nature of the Internet, any web addresses or links contained in this book may have changed since publication and may no longer be valid. The views expressed in this work are solely those of the author and do not necessarily reflect the views of the publisher, and the publisher hereby disclaims any responsibility for them.

The author of this book does not dispense medical advice or prescribe the use of any technique as a form of treatment for physical, emotional, or medical problems without the advice of a physician, either directly or indirectly. The intent of the author is only to offer information of a general nature to help you in your quest for emotional and spiritual well-being. In the event you use any of the information in this book for yourself, which is your constitutional right, the author and the publisher assume no responsibility for your actions.

Any people depicted in stock imagery provided by Thinkstock are models, and such images are being used for illustrative purposes only. Certain stock imagery © Thinkstock.

Print information available on the last page.

ISBN: 978-1-4525-7661-9 (sc)
ISBN: 978-1-4525-7662-6 (e)

Balboa Press rev. date: 09/02/2020

THE TEN METRE WALK

I sit here full of ideas and objectives, that I know many will share and many will not. At long last I've succumbed to the constant promptings of those around me, and decided to put pen to parchment. I will share my various thoughts, my views and numerous experiences. I will mention the good, the bad and the ugly, so please enjoy.

Every potential hard man, or lad looking for a reputation, will encounter trouble. The way the situation is resolved, will either enhance, or shatter, his growing reputation. We are now well and truly engrossed, in a society, hell bent on promoting anarchy.

The world we live in, is rampant with drugs and extremely dangerous people. Through working at various pubs and clubs, throughout Birmingham, I've been fortunate enough to meet, a lot of good people. Unfortunately wherever there is good, bad is not very far behind.

Within the social scene, of any city centre hot spot, there will always be disturbances. Sadly, wherever this occurs, there is always, war and violence.

I will confront the differing ways in which we make decisions and how the outcome, can be rewarding, or disastrous. I will try and explain the ten metre walk, from an ex football hooligan and doorman's point of view.

I will begin. You're in a hostile pub, working the door. You observe a group of lads, starting to get rowdy, this is Point A; you monitor the situation, knowing that in a matter of minutes, this could be a battle and an all out war.

The situation you've been watching is getting worse, your boss wants them out and so do the upset punters. The situation is quite simple, you're being paid to get them out. Now is the time to perform and do what you do best.

Here comes the thinking behind my book, Point A, you see the problem, Point B, you deal with the problem. Between A and B, you make the ten metre walk. The distance between,win or lose, fight or flight, advance or retreat.

Victory or failure hangs in the balance,what will it be? The mind set adopted, will without a shadow of a doubt, greatly influence the final outcome. If approached confidently and correctly, then excellent. This simply means folks, fall out, will be kept to a minimum. If the scenario takes a nasty twist however, the end game could be fatal.

Within that ten meter walk, reputations are carved out of stone, or in many a case,smashed like a glass chandelier. If during that short but sometimes lonely walk, you allow yourself to feel fear, then welcome to the school of life.

That fear, when controlled correctly, will turn out to be your greatest ally; and Remember people,an ally is a friend, not an enemy.

From the hooligan perspective, the ten metre walk, would be something like this.

You set out with your firm, looking for trouble. You turn the corner of the road and some two hundred yards ahead,you see the enemy coming towards you. The adrenalin, begins to rise. The anticipated violence, creates beads of dripping sweat and your body starts to get ready.

The enemy before you advance, you look for a quiver in their ranks, but all you see is an unbreakable line of men. The moment you've been waiting for is here, how will you react?

Point A, you've seen the problem and it's not going away. The problem facing you, is actually getting worse. The Two firms, are now within ten feet of each other and no ones shirking. Their faces are angry and aggressive, a perfect reflection of your own. The fight you were dreaming about last night,is no longer a dream. How will you react?

Will you be overcome with doubt and fear, which consequently ends up with you running? Or will your mind set be, one of stand and attack? Your reaction, whatever it turns out to be, represents Point B, in its fullness. Point A you see the problem, point B you deal with it.

I often think back to the crazy battles,my friends and I encountered. The pub brawls and the major fights,with rival hooligans. I can clearly recall, jumping out the back of removal vans and unleashing mayhem.

Without any doubt, the one thing I learned from my wayward younger days was, courage. Whether you're big or small, fat or thin, the common denominator everyone needs, is courage.

At some point or the other, hooligans, villains and bouncers alike, all have to put their necks on the line and demonstrate courage. When you walk the path of violence, believe you me,it takes no prisoners.

My aim and intention for this book, is not to come across as a learned educated scholar, or a twentieth century oracle. I am just man with a view and nothing special.

I am a down to earth simple man, and not someone with all the answers, to life's woes. I simply want to share experiences, that I believe we can all learn from, regardless of gender or occupation.

Call it inspiration,or call it an idea or view, born out of boredom. I honestly believe,the choices we sometimes make and decisions we often stand by,are primarily based on how we deal with pressure.

When faced with my ten metre walk scenario,it will become quite evident, it can either go very good,or it can go very bad.

I intend to somehow introduce situations, where I feel the ten meter walk is seen to its fullness. I will deal with the hard man confrontational scenarios and the every day events, where emotions and reactions, go hand in hand.

If by the end of this book, I have somehow managed to help a fellow individual, in any way at all, I have achieved my desired goal.

As a teenager leaving school, I soon learned through mixing with lads older than I, that life was no place for the weak,or faint heart-ed.

I left, Hodge Hill comprehensive school, in 1985. During the latter part of my school life, I came into contact with the known football hooligans, the infamous Zulu Warriors, of Birmingham City Football Club.

This encounter carved an impression on me, which I believe as made me a far more patient and empathetic individual.

The desire to fight and smash up pubs, as long since gone and been replaced with a desire to see young people in society, trying to maximise their potential.

The teenage years are a time where characters are built and reputations formed. My teenage years were no different, apart from the fact, I was part of a notorious hooligan gang; which terrorised football grounds around Britain.

One ingredient of the ten metre walk, shared by football hooligans and doormen alike, is courage. This particular trait, was seen to its best effects; during the hooligan period. I'll refer to this period, as the naughty days and here are a few accounts; to explain that particular side of it.

NAUGHTY DAYS

80s
WEST BROM

Saturday afternoon. Birmingham were at home to their midlands rivals, West Bromwhich Albion. The regular routine was, get into the city centre early, find a suitable pub; and wait for the away firm to land. We would normally drink In the Crown pub, Kaleidoscope, or any off side pubs that were available.

About 12:30pm, a few of us were standing out side Kaleidoscope, while the main body of the firm,was drinking inside. We were all engaged in the usual football banter and basically killing time, before the arrival of the enemy.

As we chatted away, our conversations and jesting, were suddenly interrupted. Something appeared to be kicking off near the Crown pub, and like men overcome with blood lust; we started heading towards it.

The Crown pub, was at the back of New Street station, some sixty seconds from where we stood. It was hard to see exactly what was happening, so without hesitation, we sought a closer look.

The adrenalin was already starting to build up and the hand full of us who had noticed, started walking up the road.

Everyone started putting on gloves and bringing empty bottles and pint glasses. As we neared the Albion lads, I wandered to myself, was this just a false alarm, or was this the real thing.

By now, curiosity had taken full control, and the curious walk, became a confident march, the confident march, became an excited sprint; and the excited sprint, took us to war.

We were practically falling over each other and couldn't get there quick enough. We ran towards the Crown pub and there at the top of the road, was a firm of about sixty lads. Section five, the name associated with the Albion firm,had landed.

Here we were, facing the Albion boys, while the rest of our lads, were still drinking in kaleidoscope; unaware of the situation confronting us. The usual shouting and bouncing took place, with threats of death at the fore.

This was always the true acid test. When you're face to face with the enemy, with no police in sight; the talking stops and walking starts. The bottles and glasses are always the first things to dodge and when they run out, its time to step up. The Stanley knives and coshes, always make an appearance; alongside, the plastic bottles of ammonia.

With the sizing up done and the verbal insults batted to and fro, the time for action had now come. We charged.

Punches were flying, coshes were swinging and blades were slicing. Bottles and glasses, were smashing all around you. The expected battle was going to perfection, without 'any police in sight'.

Those unfortunate enough to hit the deck, found their heads being used as footballs, but with no referee to stop play.

In-between every mad combination, came outrageous bobbing and weaving. If you stood outside punching distance, this was no guarantee of safety. Lads were swinging bats, like cricketers on a run chase, with one over to go. Pint glasses flew through the air, with the accuracy of an Eric Bristow dart. For those involved in the battle, there was certainly no hiding place.

Though a little out numbered initially, we kept on going forward. If you'd spent your wages on a nice Burberry Mac, you'd quickly regret it; blood doesn't dry clean easily.

The Albion to their credit,had played up earlier in the morning and managed to make some noises. They had come for action and ended up at the Crown pub, where they made their intentions known. Unfortunately for the Albion however, their second stop was the Zulus, and they were soon to realise, their earlier escapades, were history. The fun and games that the Albion may have had earlier,would quickly be snuffed out.

The lads who had been in kaleidoscope, missing the action, started making their way up the road. When the rest of the Zulus saw it going off, they needed no invitation to join in.

More Zulus joined the fray, their lust for battle was not being denied. Section five started to feel the full force of our anger and not surprisingly, they started to quake.

I remember seeing a large bearded chap,wearing a brown sheepskin; trying in vain to keep his lads together. However,his urges were quickly stopped, after a well-aimed left and right fist, smashed into his chin. Believe me,this chap could certainly run fast for a big man. I was pretty sure he was on the same stuff, as a drug assisted athlete. The speed of foot, was quite astonishing.

The Albion lads' who tried to stand,made very little impression and took the only option left available, scarper.

The Albion had put up a brave little stand, but that meant nothing. We pursued and punched them relentlessly,all the way, to Digbeth coach station. For section five, it had now become very serious. Their firm had split up and gone off in different directions; for those being chased, it was literally survival of the fittest.

The lucky ones got away; the not so lucky, were left knocked out on the pavement; their worse scenarios coming to pass. No quarter was asked and none was given, this was the way it was.

This unfortunately is a risk you take; when you play in the devils play ground and violence becomes your God, expect no favours.

Police vans arrived in numbers, but the damage was already done. The choices were now clear, stay and risk getting arrested, or disappear to St Andrews. I chose the latter and cheered on Birmingham City.

ALBIONS BIG RETURN

Birmingham, were playing away at West Bromwhich and in this account, I hope my explanation of the ten metre walk, is better explained.

I always enjoyed away games, you took on the feeling of a soldier going to battle, well and truly stuck behind enemy lines. You felt like a warrior, whose job was to fight for his club and not necessarily his country.

You would pace the streets of the enemy, knowing that at any moment, the bombs would start and the battle of the firms begin.

We had arranged to meet Section five, have the punch up, and then disappear as per usual. Someone had sent word to their firm, telling them we were waiting in a pub called the Lewisham; on the outskirts of town. Not only that, they were also told,the Zulus are ready for the meet.

The truth was however, when we got to the Lewisham pub, we were nowhere near ready for combat. The rest of our lads were on their way, via taxis, buses, cars and quite frankly,any means of transport available. Time keeping was never our greatest strength and on days such as these, you needed to be punctual.

We had already given section five a thrashing before, but on this occasion, all of West Bromwhich came out in numbers.

I remember being in the Lewisham pub and thinking to myself, we cant keep taking firms for granted. I sat on my stool and shook my head. I decided to stand up and then all of a sudden, a volume of deafening noise came, from outside the pub.

Section five, the Albion firm, had landed. I remember my mate saying "Elvis Elvis we've got it,we've got it" meaning, were about to go to war. Often when trouble is imminent, people always call your name twice, think about it.

We weren't prepared to get trapped inside the pub, so we rushed outside, ready for the battle.

I'll never forget, the firm that greeted us outside. Black, white, Asian, and all of the same mind set. The lads that we faced,stood in a solid line, of over two hundred and fifty. The Albion firm, stretched right across the High street. This was one of the biggest Albion turnouts, I'd ever seen. I quickly deduced,this is not just the Albion firm, no way.

When faced with a situation, where defeat is a real possibility, it's amazing how you can only see victory. This can be called wishful thinking, or to the masses; blinkered bravery. Personally,I like to think, its' your spirits way of saying "you better survive, or the consequence is death"

The battle that took place,was extremely violent, and one of the most viscous I have ever been part of. Seeing these lads in front of us, of different shapes and sizes, bottles in hand and bats at the ready, wasn't pretty. Believe me, the ten metre walk was made with much trepidation; but never the less, made.

From seeing the firm in front of us, point A, to walking towards them point B, my mind was made up. Win, loose or draw, Albion, lets have it.

Approaching a man, or a mob for that matter,who carry no weight, is easy. When you're in a situation,where you have to approach a group, who mean business, trust me; men get separated from boys.

The battle that ensued, was far from pretty. I can remember liquid being squirted in my direction, followed by a rain of bottles. I remember struggling to breathe and desperately gasping for breath. The substance that was squirted at me, literally took my breath away.

The Albion lads would charge forward in masses and be met with flurries of wild punches. I remember kicking and punching, with eyes streaming, due to the effects of the sprayed substance. Things weren't going well at all and can be summed up by the saying, 'if you fail to prepare, then prepare to fail'. I was well and truly in the devils play ground and all the gates were shut.

I recall lads having their own personal wars, everywhere you turned, the violence was unrelenting. Believe you me folks, this was heavy, heavy, violence.

We were outnumbered to the degree, where it became every man to his own devices. You didn't look for help, it was quite clear, everyone had their own personal conflicts to overcome. You just stood there,traded blows and battled for your own survival. We were being swamped from all angles, ammonia, cs gas, bleach, you name it, they had it.

Section five was out with a vengeance, and was performing accordingly. Our last encounter had not been forgotten, and for Albion, it was pay back time.

We did all we could as an out numbered firm and tried to old it together. I thought the worse was over, until I saw an orange ball of flame heading towards us, everyone ducked. After weathering the storm of ammonia, bleach and cs gas, flare guns were now being used. I thought to myself, someone obviously works for the ministry of defense.

The hatred and anger,unleashed at a fight between rival firms, is unbelievable. How there have not been more fatalities, is truly amazing. Due to the fact, we were well outnumbered, some got it worse than others; but that's the price you pay. At one stage, we managed to drag some chap to the floor, but such was the numbers we faced, we had to back off quickly. The tactics were simple,you fought at a distance.

If you let them grab old of you, you'd be quite frankly, kicked unconscious. When things get out of hand, try your best to stay on your feet. Unless you get caught, with a very decent punch, do everything you can, to remain upright.

If you end up on the ground, you'll be lucky to get back up.

As far as the Albion clash was concerned,we tried our very best to hold it together. Looking back now, I can only sigh and shrug my shoulders. We suffered very few casualties, considering the level of violence we faced. If anything at all, was learned from this encounter, it was simply this; be prepared and never let it happen again.

The police arrived in numbers and the battle died its death. I remember laying against a wall, eyes burning and struggling to breathe. I shook my head and took a deep breath. I regained my composure and went on my way. The afternoon may not have gone to plan, but at the end of the day,you live to fight another day.

It would have been easy to run and hide, but that option was never contemplated. I can honestly say, the Albion firm that met us that day, was possibly one of the most prepared firms we had met, and they performed accordingly.

Albion, were hell bent on revenge that day and all I can say is, fair play. Not taking any credit away from Albion, but I know for a fact, if we had a proper firm out that day, it would have been a battle to remember. Unfortunately we didn't,so let's just say, that's a battle we'll have to forget.

I wasn't forced into this situation,I had willingly chosen it. A decision was made and as much as I relied on my pals to have my back, I knew they also relied on me.

I remember at the time,there were a few lads, whose ten metre walk took them fleeing in the opposite direction. At the end of the day folks, we are individually responsible for our actions.

My reckless bravery could have cost me my life, while their self preservation, would prolong theirs. I dear say, when they sit down with their wife and kids; they'd have no regrets and at the end of the day, life simply moves on.

The ten metre walk, is no mystery and many a person as gone through it. Self doubt, butterflies in the gut and searching questions. Asking yourself, can I still deal with it? will I get hurt? what if this happens? I've had too much to drink etc etc etc.

Try not to chastise yourself for having these feelings, just make sure you don't succumbed to them. Whoever is reading this, please trust me when I say this. If you allow negativity into a violent situation, you put yourself, your mates and your fellow doormen, in serious danger.

You may also open up a mental can of worms, that may haunt you for a very long time.

A mental can of worms in this respect,is simply this. Lack of self confidence, self doubt and the gnawing question,can I still do this job?

Any doorman will tell you, the worse thing a member of a team can do, is run when the battle gets hot. If you're a person,who is continually engulfed in self-doubt,I can not shout this loud enough, "get your head together".

A lot of boxers who have suffered defeats, often need a win, to restore their self belief. The loss in the ring,often takes away their confidence and removes that little bounce in the stride.

Once they have re-established themselves as fighters again, they can move on and perform at another level.

Some on the other hand, fail to regain that snap and in some cases, are never the same fighter again.

CHARLTON 1987

One particular incident, that always makes me smile; is a clash we had with some Charlton fans. This took place outside a McDonald's restaurant and I always chuckle. I was only nineteen at the time, but I lived the life of a somewhat older man. There was about ten of us hanging around the city centre that evening, with very bad intentions.

Leeds and Charlton, were using our ground for a play off match. When the final whistle blew, all roads led to the direction of the city centre. It was now coming up to ten o'clock, and the match itself,was now over. A few Zulus, were walking around the city centre and taking life easy.

I remember looking down the road and noticed a group of about forty lads. I didn't need to say anything to anyone, as the eagle eyes of the Zulus had spotted them as well. Sometimes when a story is told, along the lines of,ten lads chased thirty, or fifteen run fifty, its instantly dismissed.

Anyone who understands football violence, will certainly not dismiss it. I can tell you, for an outnumbered bunch of lads, to get what hooligans call a result, is a regular occurrence. Any hooligan will tell you, he'd rather be with twenty individuals who can fight, than sixty individuals who can not.

As I said earlier, we spotted these lads coming towards us, so the battle was on. We made a little line across the road and the dancing started. We went forward in unison,with the shouts of "Zulu" deafening the ear drums. At first, these lads looked shocked more than anything else and stood still. I watched, as they were looking at each other bewildered. Then they started coming towards us, extremely cocky indeed. This overconfidence however,was soon to be destroyed.

A couple of them, got caught in the barrage of our assault, but luckily for them, they managed to escape. Some lads came out of a nearby pub and hinted at joining in, but when the punches started flying again, they chose to watch instead.

The Charlton lads regrouped and it was then, it must have dawned on them; we were greatly outnumbered. They came forward as one, with extremely mean expressions and their words to the point.

As they got closer,I heard my mate xxxx shouting to some chaps "stand boys, don't run". It was then I noticed a few pretenders amongst us. These are the sort, who like to chase people down the road, after the front lines done the hard bit. Makes me laugh really, a lot of so called tough guys, can't fight sleep in the afternoon. At the sight of a few lads ready to run, the Charlton lads gained even more confidence. At this point, I have to laugh. Out the pack of the Charlton lads, came a man, walking straight towards me. This individual, looked as cool as a cucumber and I remember thinking, oh no, its Clint Eastwood.

Believe you me, he looked just like Dirty Harry, and the recollection always brings a smile to my face. This bloke,in the midst of the mayhem,came straight towards me. The bloke didn't run,he just coolly walked towards me, without blinking an eye. He had a look on his face, which screamed out to me, "boy! I'm gunner knock you out".

On a serious note, from the time he came towards me, I knew I wouldn't run. Instead of defeating myself with thoughts of doubt, I met the challenge. Point A,I saw the problem and point B, I dealt with it.

I stated earlier,the thought pattern, between points A and B,can often determine the outcome. They can either carve a reputation out of stone, or smash it like a glass chandelier. I am in no way special, but fortunately for me, the chandelier remained intact.

As I got into punching distance, he stared menacingly at me. I remember his wide angry eyes and his two clenched fists. As far as I was concerned, the hard bit was done and I was there. I didn't stand waiting for a written invitation, I feinted with my left and threw a hay maker with my right. I must be honest, I threw the punch more in hope, than expectation, but the end result was perfect.

He was left on his back side. The lads who stood beside him, looked more shocked than me. I glanced down at him,with a, that weren't part of your script look.

When he got up, he was clutching the back of his leg, like an athlete experiencing cramp. The blokes face was certainly a picture, believe you me.

I bounced around on my toes, arms outstretched, "come on, come on then" I shouted. My adrenalin was at its peak and definitely off the scale.

We took great delight, in putting the forty strong firm, on the back foot. When the sirens sounded and the police vans arrived at the scene,we got on our toes and vanished. I glanced back at Dirty Harry and gave him a cocky smile, he never smiled back. What I had done in layman's terms was, simply confronting and standing up to my Goliath. The recollection of this event,always makes me smile. On the face of it folks, he should have frightened me to death,but fortunately for me, that wasn't the case.

It's very easy to laugh about it now, but the situation could have been oh so different. If I had allowed myself to be overwhelmed with doubt,the outcome could have been fatal.

If I had begun doubting myself and my physical ability, the result could have been somewhat disastrous. On this occasion however, I was the victor and push come to shove, that's all that matters.

Like a lot of lads growing up,I was engrossed in gangster films and the false glamour that went with them. I remember watching films like The Warriors, Wanderers and Bad Boys. I would often imagine being there. I would view the films and convince myself, I would have done this and that etc. I would of stood, whilst all the rest ran. I would be amongst those,who got back to Coney Island; watch the warriors and you'll understand what I mean.

I would have been a little superman, running through glass and catching bullets in my teeth. I'm sure you know where I am coming from.

Unfortunately, when we deal with reality, being superman; often comes at a very high price. When you watch the television, you see the action and taste the victory. The film also stirs the emotions and touches the feelings.

When you sit down to watch a movie though, there's always one thing missing. That one absent ingredient is, experiencing physical pain. No television will ever hit you with a right hand, or stick a dirty knife in your belly. These are experiences, that only come with reality, and reality I'm afraid, often disappoints.

WALSALL BATTLE

News had got round to us, that one of the lads from Birmingham, had been beaten up, by some lads from Walsall. We, and I refer to my pals at the time, had no idea who he was, or what had done, but we decided to go to Walsall; and get the matter sorted.

No one had a great deal on at the time, which made the decision easy. It was,sleepy town of Walsall, here we come. Now this was not a football associated situation, just a simple, you got one of us, we'll get plenty of you.

So off we went on the train to Walsall, about thirty lads from Birmingham. We got to Walsall and started making our way to the city centre. On the way there, we bumped into a ginger haired chap, who looked like someone in the know. "Where are your lads then?" we asked, "Word was, lads from Birmingham were coming down, but the police are on the ball", he said.

The chap went on to say, "no ones up for it". We threw a few more questions in his direction, but the answers were very much the same.

Apparently, there had been a local firm gathered, ready to cause serious damage. The police had separated them all, and apparently, they were all dispersed. The ginger haired lad departed, and left with the words of "we'll have it another time, just not now".

On hearing this, we made our way back to the train station, more than a little annoyed. We walked towards our platform and waited for our train back to Birmingham.

About twenty minutes had passed and then someone shouted "there's a firm coming" it didn't take rocket science to guess who it was. Walking towards us, were about thirty odd lads, being led by the ginger haired lad himself. He must have gone straight to the nearest pub and rustled up some followers. I dear say,the lads intention, was to send us back to Birmingham; with tail between our legs.

"Well, well", I said to myself, at least they made the effort. I watched them as they approached us. The bounce in their stride, was there for all to see. Over confidence,was exuding form every part of their body, and the arrogant stride, was there for all to see.

Our lads got together, with fists clenched,ready for the battle that lay ahead. The two mobs, stared at each other, in a little stand off; some twenty yards apart.

I can clearly recollect, the ginger haired lads, cocky and smirking face. Along side him, were some very unsavory looking characters as well. The Walsall chaps stood staring, whilst making a lot noise. They must of thought to themselves, this is a cake walk and going to be an easy nights work. They looked at us,while clutching silver Stanley knives.

Here I was, the warriors and wanderers revisited, only this time, it wasn't a film.

The scene now before me,was very much reality. The lads that stood before me, were very much reality, and the lust for blood, was certainly a reality.

Our lads were in a strong line and their lads appeared to be in a strong line. Our chaps knew why we came to Walsall, and it wasn't to marvel at their famous illuminations. Zulus came for war and believe me, Zulus wanted war.

The white guys in their firm shouted "were gunner kill you" and the black guys shouted something similar. Lets just say folks, a few Jamaican expletives, were definitely thrown about.

"Come on then, lets have it", was shouted at the top of our voices, accompanied with the well established "Zulu"and we charged.

The Walsall chaps, looked like rabbits caught in head lights and ran quicker than Usein Bolt. We gave chase, picking up discarded weapons along the way. I remember seeing, a Burberry hat and some designer caps, laying on the floor. We ran them right out the train station and into the wet and windy street. When we got outside, police vans were already in attendance, with sirens blaring.

The presence of the local police,had the desired effect and our pursuit ceased. There was another twenty odd Walsall lads, waiting near the train station. The thought of entering the station,was obviously unappealing.

We engaged in the usual verbal, but with police in attendance, the battle was effectively over. We begrudgingly headed back to our platform, shaking our heads as we did. If they'd stood toe to toe, the matter would have been resolved. Failing in their ten metre walk, just left us at a loose end. With nothing left to wait for and the adrenalin long gone, we caught the first available train back to New St, and called it a day.

Within this Walsall scenario, the ten metre walk is seen in both lights. As the Walsall lads were making there way to the platform, they knew exactly what lay ahead.

On entering the station, they must have felt very confident and definitely up for it. Over confidence, coupled with bravado,turned out to be their undoing.

I would imagine, they discussed what they were going to do us and they probably bragged and boasted one to another. The Walsall chaps, probably mocked us and were already celebrating their victory. I believe they saw it as a mere formality and another tick in the box.

When they stood before us, those who initially boasted, were given a serious reality check. They obviously allowed their negative thoughts,to greatly out weigh their positive thoughts.

The fight or flight response was triggered,with the flight response,taking precedence. This wasn't a situation where they were vastly outnumbered, we were evenly matched. The fact they all seemed to possess weapons, gave them a slight edge. Their initial outward appearance, was one of confidence, but within the grey matter of the brain, this wasn't registering.

During the stand off, numerous threats and curses were exchanged. Based on the way the events unfolded, the impact on them,obviously outweighed the impact on us.

That Walsall escapade, though amusing at the time, can be life changing for many. Sadly,there are those, whose reality and moment of truth, as been far to overwhelming to deal with.

My reality had arrived. Managing to hold myself together, coupled with the fact I had good lads around me, meant I got through it. Sadly there are those, whose reality as left them embarrassed,or in some cases, dead.

BHANGRA REVENGE

When someone is unjustly attacked, revenge is often sought. When it's a person who doesn't like being attacked, revenge isn't an issue, it's a done deal.

I was working the door at a Bhangra gig, which is an Asian type dance event. After being attacked at this venue, the fate for those involved, wasn't very pretty.

The background to what took place, is written in the chapter called Dangerous lady. The outcome however, I will deal with now.

It was a Friday evening and all the lads were gathered together. We had arranged to meet at a certain location, get tooled up and then go to war.

This was to be the final showdown, between two warring mobs and a termination, to an abundance of empty threats. Numerous Insults, were being thrown in our direction and that only meant one thing.

War was certainly inevitable, with people getting seriously hurt and badly bruised. We had already discussed the plan of attack and the time to stop talking, had now come. It was time put it into practice, what we did best and teach some would be pretenders, a harsh lesson. The talking had been done, the decisions had been made and retribution, was now firmly at the door.

Here we were. Hammers, bats, blades and machetes, we were ready for action. As far as I was concerned, the end result was inevitable and the noisy lads, would be silenced.

We hired a min bus and blackened out the windows with bin liners. With fifteen in the van and another ten in cars, we were off.

We set off to war like workmen, with laughing, joking and endless high jinx. We talked about every day things and clarified the ins and outs, of the task that lay ahead. When we were about a mile away from the battle ground, all the talking stopped. Everyone present,entered there own little private zone. People focused themselves on the task ahead and the violent job at hand.

The climax to weeks of threats and brags, were going to be dealt with. The moment of truth was waiting and we were eager to greet her.

I remember parking up in a backstreet off xxxx road and off to war we went. The enemy had met and were congregating in local cafes. All week they had been arrogantly saying, "Where are your boys then? we'll cut them to pieces".

Big boasts,form big mouths I thought. Their day of reckoning would soon be upon them and then the boasting would stop.

As we ran towards the cafes, I looked at the firm we had put together and smiled. The boys are coming and wars coming with us. We came to the cafe door and the hinges flew off,at the force of a twenty stone kick (Big T). We were ready and so were they, the battle started.

I remember the place going dark, someone had smashed the light bulbs. Why they did it,I don't know, but whatever the reason, it never stopped the carnage that followed.

Punches, slashes, head buts and batons, everything was going in. The mob we faced,was made up of lads who thought they were untouchable. The mob was largely made up of, brothers, cousins and taxi drivers. They certainly never expected an army of Zulus to land and when we did, they felt it.

These lads had bitten off,more than they could chew and we were relentless in our destruction. "Zulu" was shouted.

The enemy made exits that never existed and their gang fled. I remembered the words, "where are your boys then, we'll cut them to pieces," I shook my head and laughed.

Some of us involved,were known to the local community, so the balaclavas stayed put. Our firm ran back to our vehicles and cars halted in our path. We swarmed across the road, with weapons still in our hands. The job was now done, we had accomplished our objective. We made sure everyone was accounted for and headed back to our chosen location.

The majority of us who were there, went for a well earned drink. We didn't brag, we didn't boast, we just laughed our heads off. To all present, this was business as usual. We were hooligans, we were Zulu Warriors.

Whenever I visit this particular area,I always laugh to myself. Some of the lads we dealt with,are still giving the people of the community hell. Some people, unfortunately never learn. It wasn't so long ago,these same chaps, who are now causing trouble; were running down the road in sheer terror.

Racism

Any genuine person,should have no time for racists. People who go out their way to disrupt people's lives, because of skin colour. These people, are sick,prehistoric and very very ignorant. Some firms make a point of touting themselves as right wing and embrace it with a passion.

Birmingham city's firm,is renowned for the black,white and Asian mix. With a name like Zulu, what can I say. Aston villas firm on the other hand, is the total opposite.

I remember finishing work one night and heading to my old local, the Rock pub. On arrival, standing outside the pub, were six of my pals. I could see they were upset, so I asked the question "whats up" They told me, some villa fans were in a club up the road, called the Morris and making Nazi salutes. "Their giving it the Adolph Hitler's Elvis". They said.

This by itself was no surprise, what was surprising however, was the token black guy with them. My friends went on to tell me, this particular chap,was joining in. What possesses a man, to sit in the midst of racist banter and laugh at it. People are singing insulting songs about your history and you smile.

After a minute of the conversation, I knew exactly what would be decided. This was a time, when fighting was second nature to all of us, so the decision was easy. We got ourselves prepared and made our way up the road. What had taken place,had upset everyone. The Morris club was only two minutes away,so a stand would have to be made. The closer we got to the Morris club, the angrier we all became.

There was quite a few of them drinking, so we decided to wait. We stood by the car park entrance and within seconds, out came the singing racists. "Lets have it" was yelled and the punches hit home.

Some shocked by our assault, flew down the road like eagles, without a second look. The ones who momentarily stood, quickly regretted it and ran towards the petrol station.

We gave chase, punching and kicking as we did. Some lad's unsuccessfully tried to blend in with the watching crowd. Someone should have told them, designer gear, stands out, especially against sixty year old domino players. Young men, thinking they could hide behind old men, shame on you.

For the lack of common sense and insulting our intelligence, they were beaten again. The lads who sought refuge in the petrol station,were also jumped on. Here we were, in the middle of a petrol station, kicking lads for fun, Cars were pulling in, and then reversing out a break neck speed.

A taxi driver I knew called Mac, pleaded with us to stop. Mac even let some of them jump into his cab. I screamed at him "Mac, what you playing at " ? but he chose to help them.

How ironic, thirty minutes earlier, they were making racist remarks, and now, their saviour,is a black man. Mac later told me, he dropped the lads off at Aston and they kicked dents in his car. He said "if I'd known they were such racists, I wouldn't have helped them". I just laughed and said "serves you right Mac".

These events, shows the foolishness of prejudice. The people you choose to hate and ridicule,can turn out to be the ones who save your life. I could never understand,how someone could target a group of people, as being worthy of hatred; simply because of skin colour.

I see how the growing immigration problem and the drain on the countries resources, can breed anger. What I can't understand however, is how you can allow that anger,to develop into hate.

When I watch documentaries about world war II, I see photos of numerous graves and cemeteries. The thousands of troops, who lost their lives, defending a country against Nazi invasion. These people,joined a viscous war and gave the ultimate gift of all, their lives. They fought a German army, who fashioned itself on Sieg Heil, swastikas and mass murder.

I often wander,what some of these old soldiers would make of this generation. How would they feel, if they saw lads marching around the country, making Nazi hand signs. Not only this,but promoting the same views, of the nineteenth century enemy.

Ask yourself a question. If your kids were dieing,would you refuse them an operation,from the Asian surgeon? Would you let your teeth decay, because the dentist is an Indian? If your mother stopped breathing, would you refuse mouth to mouth, because the paramedic is black?

My daughters are ten and four as I write this and their best friends are white. When they play together, I see it as something beautiful and I'm proud to have brought them up this way. If you see it as something to be ashamed of, how sad and ignorant you are.

A pal of mine,was telling me about some trouble he had with some Leicester fans, in 2004. He went on to tell me, when things got very bad, some of them started giving it the 'black this and black that' abuse.

My first question was "didn't they have black guys with them?" his answer was "yes". I said "you mean to say, their dropping the racist vibe, with black guys beside them"? his answer was "yes".

25

I have been to Leicester on a number of occasions and always noticed an ethnic mix, what happened here was very surprising.

The eighties, is the era I remember and the one where the guys beside you, were genuine. If this is the type of loyalty and respect lads are giving each other nowadays, I'm glad I'm no longer part of it.

RACISM is a specific form of discrimination and exclusion faced by minority ethnic groups.

RACISM is based on a false belief, that some races are inherently superior to others, because of their skin colour, nationality, ethnic or cultural background.

RACISM deprives people of their basic human rights, dignity and respect.

BATTLEING TOTTENHAM 2003

L ife never ceases to amaze me, I have seen big men felled by small, fat men felled by thin and ugly brutes done by pretty boys. The next revelation I will bring, is nothing new; but boy oh boy, it even surprised me.

It was Saturday afternoon, Birmingham were playing at home to Tottenham. I was sitting in the family stand,and applauding a good performance. I sat alongside my brother Ray and my nephew Leon. We had just won 1-0, the perfect start to the season, and a good excuse for a celebratory drink.

The match had kicked off early, so by two o'clock, I was at a loose end. I said goodbye to my brother and his son and went on my merry way. Outside the ground, I bumped into some old Zulu acquaintants and set off for what I hoped, was a very swift drink; how wrong I was.

We headed towards the city centre, with football issues at the fore; but this was soon to change. I remember a lad running towards us and excitedly saying, some Tottenham fans are making their way to the city centre. Apparently, these guys were making a lot of noise, as they did.

On hearing this, I thought oh well 'there goes the quiet drink. I had not been active in the hooligan front, for a good while, but I knew I would be called upon for assistance. My pal said to me "there was only one thing we can do, catch them up and teach them a lesson".

Part of me wasn't that bothered at first, but being with some of the old boys, got my adrenalin going. The buzz I once felt,started flowing through my body again, and all the old feelings of the eighties, came rushing back.

As we walked towards the city centre,there were police vans in abundance. This was nothing new to be honest,as we were playing a London side.

I say not a great deal surprises me, but what took place in the next half hour,certainly did. We stepped up the pace and kept are eyes peeled for the Tottenham group.

We got to Digbeth, which is roughly ten minutes away from the city centre and it was there we spotted our foe. There were two pals ahead of me and they wasted no time in making there feelings known. As we approached this group, I immediately thought, these guys look like the real deal.

Prior, to actually coming head to head, there had been mention of a big black guy, in a green T shirt. Apparently, he was making his presence felt and lo and behold,he was there. Along side him, was a stocky white guy and it was clearly obvious, these were their governors.

As we approached them, I saw the white guy flapping his arms towards my pal. This was done to basically say, lets see what you've got. Here we were, facing a bunch of thirty, rather loud Tottenham fans. They had made a point, of slipping the escort and making their own way from the ground. They were obviously,hell bent on trouble and wanted the whole world to know it.

Their intentions were crystal clear and they even made a line, in the middle of the street. I thought to myself, 'OK Elvis,were going to war '.

These lads stood there, looking menacing and ready for action. Anyway, here came the ten metre walk. As I got closer to them, off came the sun glasses and on came my cap. The thought pattern, between point A and point B, was crystal clear. This is a fight and I'm ready for whatever you throw.

Initially, these lads stood like trees and showed no signs of budging. Our chaps started getting closer and closer. I noticed a couple of their chaps, looking increasingly worried. In my head, I thought to myself, these lads aren't as tough as they look. "Come on then, Zulu" was shouted, and to my honest amazement, they fled. At this point, many will be thinking 'here we go, another we ran them down the road comment' but believe you me, this is exactly what happened.

When I wrote about the West Bromwich return, I made it quite clear, things never went well. I made no attempt at all, to hide, or dilute the fact. I'm not in the business of story telling, what I write, is exactly as it was.

We caught hold of one lad, who to be totally honest, got a half heart-ed beating. This was purely because, we were all in a state of shock and bewilderment.

To see lads of that size, run without even throwing a punch, shocked me, it genuinely shocked me. Don't get me wrong, I'm certainly not complaining, but I was definitely staggered.

When we regrouped, we all just looked at each other and said, "did that just happen"? How could blokes that size, move so quick. This was a situation, where you had to see it, to believe it. Looking back now, I see it simply as a surprise and nothing more. Further more, those involved, lived to see another day and that's what really matters.

Running isn't unique and at some time in our lives, we've all done it. Not only did these lad run, they sacrificed their pal, to a potential pack of wolves.

Considering the situation he was in, he got away very lightly. I think everyone was more shell shocked than anything else and as a consequence, lost their appetites. It was basically the Tottenham clash in 2003 and various incidents on the local doors, that sparked my thinking. There were also numerous things that took place, during my day to day life, that also raised my awareness.

I quickly realised, the mind set adopted is crucial. No matter how rough and tough you look as an individual. If your heads not right, you'll fall short. A gang of twenty, will chase a gang of fifty and that's a given.

MILLWALL

Milllwall, were always regarded, as a ferocious fighting firm. Their reputation proceeded them and they always came for the battle. The first time I encountered them personally, was in the eighties and I wasn't disappointed. Some battles are quickly forgotten, but those of eighties, are often remembered.

It was an evening kick off and for weeks, the bad boys of the city were buzzing. The match couldn't come quick enough and for many, this was definitely the big one.

All the lads met in Boogies Wine bar, which was controlled by Birmingham City and waited.

The expectation of the night was immense and everyone was of the same mindset. Lads were working themselves into frenzy, like a champagne cork ready to explode. We knew what had to be done, all that was left now, was the emergence Millwall.

The Zulu scouts had their eyes pealed, whilst monitoring the incoming trains. Groups of lads were outside The Crown pub, which was very near to New St Station. Other lads just waited in the wings, all with the same violent intention. Everything was in place, everything was now set and everyone was ready.

Time stood still. Every time you looked at your watch face, the hands stood still. All the lads wondered to themselves, where are they ?

The Millwall were coming, there was no doubt about that, but when would it be?

Phone calls were constantly being made. Every time the receiver went down, you thought this is it. The false alarms and wrong information, was proving to be very frustrating. The waiting around added to the intensity of the evening. All eyes,were firmly fixed on New St Station. Lads were drinking their beer,on automatic pilot, taste not registering. This was no evening, for the weak or faint heart-ed. Everyone present, was there for one solitary reason and that was war.

It felt like a boxer,waiting for an opponent,while the opponent, deliberately delayed his entry.

The clock was ticking and the emergence of Millwall, was extremely close at hand. We looked towards New St Station and finally got the news we were waiting for. One of our scouts, charged through the door of Boogies and shouted the magic words, "Millwall are here!"

We flew through the doors at break neck speed, nearly taking the hinges off, as we did. The first thing I noticed,was an eighteen stone bloke,charging in our direction. The large man, with fists clenched,came at us,like a wild raging bull.

That tactic might have worked at other grounds, but it wasn't about to work here. The amount of bottles and punches that rained down on him, made him sound like a techno beat.

Across the road, the Millwall stood together. The Zulus charged and the battle exploded. Unsurprisingly,the battle started off toe to toe, with no one giving any ground. We had expected a war and we weren't being denied.

On this particular night however, we were relentless in our ferocity. Like the Sean Connery movie, Highlander, 'there could only be one survivor'. This was our moment,we had waited far too long, for any other result, but victory.

Carving knives, coshes, bottles and blades. Anything that caused pain,was utilised. Our adrenalin was focused, on the lads in front of us. The Millwall ranks,slowly started to break. They must have wondered, what on earth, as hit them; as being on the back foot, wasn't part of the Millwall script. This was the Zulus, at their best. We were making a significant statement and sending out a lasting message.

We ran some of their lads, back towards the station. I passed bodies lying on the floor, knocked out cold. Heads were being kicked like footballs, with eyes wide open. There were discarded meat cleavers and bread knives, wrapped up in London news papers. These were the hooligan weapons of war, owners long departed.

Some of the Millwall,ran in the direction of the Crown pub, only to be faced with more Zulus, baying for blood.

The vicinity around Boogies and the Crown, had been a vicious battle ground. The area, was simply one of total anarchy. Even the local police, seemed reluctant to enforce, the powers of arrest. I can clearly remember an officer, turning a blind eye, as a lad got bashed with a bike chain. Maybe he realised, on this dark and dangerous night, some things, are best unnoticed.

To be honest, I didn't blame him at all. We live in a very mixed up world, and sometimes, discretion is the better part of valour.

LEEDS

An event which made national news, was the riot at St Andrews. Birmingham, entertained Leeds United that day and what a day it was.

The level of the violence, that took place that Saturday, was truly frightening. When I look back to that day, I thank the almighty God in heaven, I am still alive. There are many today, who could quite easily have been maimed, or trampled underfoot, by rampaging horses.

One particular incident, had me thanking almighty God. How on earth I got out of it, was truly a miracle.

It was half an hour before kick off and I was walking around the ground. I was avoiding the numerous baton charges and all the blatant threats from the local police.

I recall walking down a road with my pals, and right ahead of us, was a mob of very angry Leeds fans. To be totally honest, this shouldn't have surprised me, as I was slap bang, by the away end.

I remember saying to a pal " this is well on top mate, the away end, I must be potty".

Any way, here I was, with a group of unknown lads. My head was saying run, my heart was saying stand. I looked about me and thought, OK, there's a good few of us here. Unfortunately compared to the Leeds however, we were merely a few.

The Leeds fans were not famous for there racial tolerance and their language certainly reinforced it. "Come on then, you black b" they said. All around me were chants of "you black this, you black that" and I'm pretty sure, you can imagine the rest. It certainly wasn't Emmerdale farm language. Well well, here we go. We never came for a crash course in tractor driving, we came for war. Bang, off it went.

I remember kicking out like a maniac and making sure I stayed on my feet. The police were coming from every where, while the rival fans, slugged it out. I remember a group of Leeds fans,going for a pal called Fat Errol. They were shouting the usual insults, amongst the black this and black that.

I remember thinking, Ezza their not to happy with you mate. Deep down, I thought, if any one can pull this off, Fat Errol can. Even though we were outnumbered,we fought and battled away. Bottles, pies, rocks and cans, every thing that could be thrown, was thrown.

All fighting technique, went out the window. There was no combinations and fancy foot work. This was simple,punch,punch and punch some more. The police did their thing and tried to restore some peace, we did our thing and disappeared from the scene.

I remember being chased by a police horse and jumping a garden wall. The pursuing officer,pulled on his reins and glared towards me. The officer knew he could go no further, unless he fancied jumping through someone's living room window.

I laughed and held my hands out. The officer obviously annoyed, looked at me and said "I'd love to see your black head, underneath my horse hooves" charming I thought.

Comments like this were quite common and I never doubted for a minute, he meant it. After watching a recent documentary, called The Secret policeman on BBC1, I see not a great deal as changed.

Inside the ground everyone had a different story to tell, the atmosphere was truly electric. Lads talked about the different battles they had, before and after the game. looking back now, it was as if a spirit of violence,had descended on all of us. The lust for blood was frightening and it seemed as though, evil was a necessity.

What I have written, is a personal recollection, of a frightening situation. I consider myself extremely fortunate,to have got away, unscathed. What took place that day, wasn't pretty at all. The violent events, both before and after that game, could fill its own book.

There's no glory whatsoever, in anything that happened that day. The Birmingham-Leeds riot, was a terrible day for football and a tragic day for a young boy; who sadly lost his life. I have made a point, not to dwell on the details of my past. My genuine aim, is to positively help a fellow individual, in any way I can.

A lot of the incidents I have referred to, took place in the eighties and are very much done and dusted. The clashes I've re referred to, are only being used as examples and nothing else.

I don't want to appear, or come across, as a man who glories in past wars. Maturity and the good things in life, make you realise, what is and what isn't important. I consider myself extremely fortunate, to have come out in one piece; and can see the faces, of all my five children. Christina, Jaidon, Alana, Jacob and Luke.

The hooligan days, were a season of my life, where the final whistle as definitely been blown. My life now, is that of a born again Christian and I have never been so happy. Peace

A wonderful quote....

"The person that loses their conscience
as nothing left worth keeping"

HOOLIGANS VS DOORMEN

Hooliganism, as long been regarded as the match day syndrome. It is as been said, many people conduct themselves lawfully throughout the week, and on match day, the monster comes out. This is only true to a certain degree. Personally, I think it only relates to the part time hooligans.

I remember on many occasions, lads would meet during the week days and sort out violent issues. These issues in question, weren't even football related. Nonetheless, they would be dealt with, with the same zeal, as a match day encounter.

The 'Bhangra revenge' episode, was a catalogue of events, where the end result; was lads being severely dealt with, who lets face it, cared very little about football.

Hooligan culture,exists throughout the week, but only comes to light,during football events. To imply a decent person, suddenly becomes a maniac on match day, is very shallow. What that interpretation implies is, if a situation occurred, which was potentially violent, unless it's match day,it will end with hand shakes. The individuals involved in a heated encounter,will graciously turn the other cheek. Are we suggesting, individuals involved in hooliganism,are actually Jekyll and Hyde characters.

They are actually unbalanced individuals,who have warped, schizophrenic natures. I have never really subscribed to this view, nor am I overly convinced. Using my past as an example, if you're violent on a Saturday, then there's every chance, you'll be violent, Monday to Friday as well.

I must admit however, some bouncers don the black suit and become different individuals. This could be a psychological problem, or possibly, some hidden issue from childhood. I will humbly say, this particular area, is best left to the experts. I am no psychologist, so I will keep an open mind and leave this argument alone.

There are many hot headed bouncers, who sadly carry this emotion, into their place of work. The aggressive doormen I've met, often have problems, with switching off. As a consequence, they never seem happy. Regardless of their surroundings I.e. quiet country pub, or a busy West end night club.

Many door staff you talk to, simply find chilling out, very difficult. What I often find interesting is, security isn't always responsible, for this bad behavior. Many were like this, before they even entered the realm of security. Nowadays, security is a lot harder to get into. If you're caught doing something you shouldn't be, your manager can get severely fined.

The fact remains. Bad apples, get mixed into the bag, right alongside the good ones. I pray your journey folks, in whatever field of security you enter, is safe. "May God be your protector"

Amen

Characteristics of the HOOLIGAN   Characteristics DOORMEN

Characteristics of the HOOLIGAN	Characteristics DOORMEN
Tribal	Tribal
Single-minded	Single minded
Unwavering	Unwavering
Violent when necessary	Violent when necessary
Loyal	Loyal
Irrational	Rational
Anarchistic	Hooliganism

When you've been actively involved, in both hooliganism and bouncing, you understand the differences. While similarities do exist, the hooligan as no middle ground. When you set out on match day, you exist for the tear up, and little else matters. Whether you're a father, boyfriend, or good husband, nothing comes before the clash. You have one objective for the day and that is violence.

The violent desire of the hooligan, is what separates them, from the genuine doormen. A hooligan desires violence, a doorman desires peace. On match day, from the moment you get out your bed, you put your designer clothes on, and off you go. You know exactly what lies ahead, as you open your front door and slam it behind you, you're intentions are clear.

The desire to unleash the wicked devil, is your sole priority. This emotion, comes before your job, your family and your life. Regardless of the match result, your goal is crystal clear, a meeting with the rival firm.

The average man, will ask the question, "what makes grown men, act like children and fight each other" ? An answer that springs to mind, is simply this (Tribal Warfare) From the dawn of time, mankind as always found a reason to fight.

Whether it is the country you're from, or the skin colour you possess. Any thing, that separates one human being form another, is often a sufficient reason for war.

If you have ten Caucasian men in a room, skin colour isn't an issue. If the ten men of the same colour enter an heated argument, then origin becomes the issue. I.e. English, Irish, Scottish or Welsh. When a catalyst for confrontation as been found, along with a reason for assault, mankind's nature does the rest.

Some answers, are more complicated than they need to be. Football hooliganism, is no more a mystery, than the loch Ness monster. Hooliganism exists, because war and hate exists.

From the murderous slaying of Abel, at the hands of a jealous Cane, violence and sin exists. The nature of fallen man, is that of conflict, war and confrontation. Turn on you're television and look at the news channel. From my limited knowledge of life, conflict as always existed.

Governments don't like easy answers. Members of parliament, study for years and when asked a question, their answer is often ambiguous. A simple and straight forward answer,makes the boffin feel uneasy. The graduate, now finds themselves, on the same intellectual level, as the uneducated man.

Doorstaff

Unlike the hooligan, most doormen don't go to work, in the hope of a good punch up. The genuine doorman, realises, that violence isn't something to cherish. A fight isn't something desired, or welcomed with open arms.

Violence in any form, can be frightening. Violence can also be life changing and in some cases fatal. When a doorman goes to work, he knows the risks that accompany the job. Based upon his knowledge, he's wise enough to know,war isn't something to desire.

The doorman's role, is the total opposite to that of the hooligan. The doorman stands at the front of house,or wherever he's positioned. The doorman is faced with the task, of stopping and spotting any potential trouble.

The hooligan on the other hand, will go out of his way, to look for trouble and if it's not spotted, start it. If a bouncer spots a group of potential trouble makers, approaching the door, his first thought is protection. The doorman won't allow them entry into the pub and the reasons are simple. Should hell explode in their establishment, he may well get badly burnt.

When you've worked a few doors, experience teaches you, avoid hell and most definitely its angels. The hooligan on the other hand, spots potential trouble and sees it as a bull's-eye. The thought of shying away, is totally dismissed and the thought of confrontation, is totally embraced.

The genuine doorman,welcomes and treats all punters alike. A weekend reveler, often feels discriminated against,especially when refused entry. Not speaking on behalf of all doormen, but this only happens,if good reason is found.

The tribal connection between doormen, is basically, us against them. The doorman's enemy, is usually the drunkard punters, who go out their way, to cause and provoke trouble. Decent punters, are whole heartedly welcomed.

The football hooligan is single minded and unwavering in time of battle. If a firm of one hundred lads, meets another firm of one hundred lads, all involved, have the same intention.

The doorman and punter relationship, is not always straight forward. The doorman must sift through the good and anticipate the bad. If you let one hundred punters in the pub, five can be potential enemies. The other ninety-five,can be very decent people, but that five however,can make life extremely difficult.

Similarities, both hooligans and doormen share alike. Loyalty, courage and camaraderie.

Loyalty

The hooligan, relies a 100% on the loyalty of his lads, In time of battle. You know for sure, your back is covered. If you're involved in a punch up, you expect the friends beside you, to battle. If someone's in a sticky situation, then it's your duty, as a friend, to see them unstuck. I know it's a lot easier said than done, but at the end of the day, you stand and fall together.

I stated in the earlier chapters, it's better to have a firm of thirty courageous lads, than a frightened firm of sixty. Thankfully, most of the chaps I worked alongside, were decent guys. When I was a hooligan, I had my firm for support. As a doorman,I had my team. I can look back now and make a honest statement. In regards to all the friends and doormen I have worked with,we had proper loyalty.

I can sincerely look back and smile. There's almost a sense of relief. Coming through the numerous skirmishes,as certainly left lasting memories. My friends and I,followed a simple motto, "In times of trouble,we stand and fall together"

When the enemy stands before you, with bottles and weapons in hand, the bravado stops. For those who boasted about their so called past victories, their moment of truth as arrived. Weeks of planning, can be destroyed in an instant and a persons reputation, gone up in smoke.

There are numerous stories and accounts,written in the books of hooliganism. Some are fabricated to build up a reputation, while others, are too ridiculous to believe. One thing is for sure and many lads will testify to this. A smaller firm, that is easily out numbered, as toppled many a bigger firm. When nobodies budging, then as a small firm, you're dangerous. You can quite literally, take on any thing. When you collectively charge forward, those opposing you, will often falter. If a large firm, ends up running,this can be seen as shameful and very embarrassing.

It's been said, every dog as its day and that's very true. Over the years,every firm as had an off day. For whatever reason, things just didn't go to plan. Was it arrogance, or over confidence? Who knows, you simply never performed on the day.

Doormen, often have to deal with being outnumbered. The experience and feelings are very much the same. If your dealing with an issue, which becomes bigger and more ferocious than anticipated, your metal is tested.

A situation could emerge,where you believe you're dealing with three punters. When the situation starts to get serious, you quickly realise, there's anther ten to deal with. If a situation like this occurs,you stand or fall together. Just like the philosophy of the hooligan, you stand together. The doorman and hooligan alike, detest those who run off. If a fight breaks out in the pub, the door team, collectively perform as a unit. The doorman that disappears into the toilet, or slips out the exit door, will have a very short career.

In a lot of cases, the punters are bigger than the door men. On observation alone, this may seem worrying. Regardless of their appearance and size, should trouble kick off, a job still as to be done.

I made reference in the chapter 'Naughty days', confronting a firm, or someone you can easily deal with, is easy. Dealing with a situation, where the result is far from obvious, is the acid test. It is moments like these, your courage will come to light.

The fact remains, when a situation gets uncomfortable and violence is imminent, you need courage. I hope all those who are reading this book, are not put off. I'm simply making you aware, your courage will indeed be tested. To all security personnel out there, please stay safe.

ARISTOTLE

The coward calls the brave man rash; the rash man calls him a coward.

Unwavering approach

Any hooligan knows, in an atmosphere that seems unsettled, expect the unexpected. The hooligan as no confusion,when it goes bang, he knows exactly what to do.

When things get serious, there's no quarter asked and none given. If you meet the enemy, then quite frankly, you're looking to do some damage. I've seen many situations,where men have hit the floor and taken a savage beating.

When a fight would break out, it was your objective, to do to them, what they would do to you. The word merciless, springs to mind. I remember guys, being kicked and stamped on; their pleas of mercy, would fall on death ears. When things get nasty, asking for mercy isn't going to work. You're only saviour, is the flashing blue lights of the police. Hooligans are very unwavering and in such a serious business, you can't afford to be anything less.

The doorman's job, is built around decision making. Some take time, while others are instantly made. If a doorman sees a group of punters and they look like trouble, he knocks them back. When the inevitable debating starts and the verbal threats are thrown, he sticks to his guns. "You're not coming in and that's final"

There's no room for debating, the decisions been made. There's no backing down from you, or the team. If from that point onwards, things take another course and get violent, then the doorman, should be mentally prepared to deal with it.

When you see lads approaching the door, a refusal of entry, can go numerous ways. A doorman's experience, teaches him to be prepared for all scenarios. If the worse scenario occurs, then your more than ready, to deal with it.

When any issue at all, is sorted peacefully, then thank God.

In such a turbulent job, doormen can't be too pliable and too easily swayed. When you make a decision, stick to it, unless of course, it's blatantly wrong.

In a cases such as this, where you know you're wrong, simply acknowledge it. You wont necessarily appear weak. When you humble yourself, it often works in your favour. Especially in the long run.

The hooligan as his role, the doorman as his

Trouble in the pub	Doorman deals with it
Trouble at the front of house	Doorman deals with it
Drunkenness	Doorman deals with it
A fight	Doorman deals with it
Personal assaults	Doorman deals with it
Confrontation	Doorman deals with it

The hooligan and the doorman, have to be unwavering in their approach. When a decision as to made, you make it. If something needs to be dealt with, you deal with it.

RUGBY PLAYERS VS DOORMEN

I was asked to take part in a charity rugby match, in aid of cancer research.

My first reaction was 'yeah yeah love to', then after my first training session, I regretted it. I was left thinking, me and my big mouth. When I actually joined the team, who were made of up bouncers and bruisers, there was only three weeks training before the match.

My first session consisted of, how to tackle stationary opponents. Week two was tackling opponents,who were running. I knew the skill and timing involved in tackling, were crucial. A good tackle, could be the difference between hospital or elation.

I certainly didn't fancy the hospital, so I gave the coach my utmost attention.

After the tackling drills were completed, we made little circles. Everyone started throwing the balls around at each-over. We tried to keep the momentum going, for as long as we possibly could. I hadn't thrown a rugby ball for years and was finding the entire experience brilliant, I felt like a kid again.

With the drills drawing to a close, the coach told us to get ready for a mini game. He emphasised the fact,the drills practiced, would be seen to their best effect, during a game.

Two teams of seven were picked, while other players, watched on the side lines. The coach reinforced to the players, we were only practicing, so try and enjoy. Before the whistle was blown, he reinforced to everyone "keep your heads together boys and don't be silly"

Within the first fifteen seconds, 'stop!' was shouted. The organiser of the match Tony Williams, had been elbowed in the nose and after a quick mop up, the match resumed. For want of a better phrase, I think crash, bang, wallop, sums up the early exchanges. We were flying into each other with the zeal of professionals, but with the technique of amateurs.

A young lad called Andy, was on the opposing side; he not only looked like, Jonah Lomu, he ran like the man as well. The first run he made, resembled skittles in a bowling alley. I laughed when I heard him say. "Is that all you have to do, run with the ball, to the other end"? The innocence of youth I thought.

We also had a big lad on our side, a good friend of mine,Terry Andrews. Just like Andy, when he ran with the ball, he also took some stopping.

After ten minutes of constant battering, a water break was taken. After everyone was refreshed, a further fifteen minutes was played. With fatigue now setting in, we concentrated on skill and the ball was thrown around much better.

The rugby being played,was actually good to watch. The two sides continued to give it their all and after the winning try was scored, we all left the field exhausted.

I was battered about with an intensity, I had never felt before, but I loved it. This was the end of my first session and with big Andy's footprint still in my chest, along with Alan Blundell's, I went to the bar. This was the first session out the way and my body wasn't pleased at all. I hadn't played rugby since leaving school and had totally forgotten just how hard it was.

The second session was somewhat of a technical affair. The coach of Yardley District Rugby Club, decided to lend a hand. He gave us the ins and outs of the line out, but with two weeks to kick off, it was too little, too late. How on earth we were supposed to learn the line out and other technical drills,was simply beyond us.

Some of the Yardley players, were watching from the sidelines, and without doubt, they were inwardly laughing. What we were trying to learn, was a total mystery. Shouted commands of 'break right, break left', seemed like another language and to be honest, we looked like the novices we were. This particular session was proving to be pointless and trust me; a few of us were getting very disgruntled. We were running around like headless chickens. Not only did we look lost, our personal pride was now being dented.

The organisers of the match, were called away for a television Interview. The match was a charity event and alongside the rugby, there was a forty eight hour, treadmill and rowing challenge. With two players now gone, we decide to abandon the drills and get down to what we all wanted; a mini match.

Two teams of seven were picked and just like the first session, we did what we knew best and that was crash, bang and wallop.

The third session was a non event and we spent the afternoon, watching our opponents play a friendly.

Sunday 30, 08, 04 the showdown:

The big day had now arrived. Our limited techniques and skills, were now on public display. Before the match started, a minutes silence was observed, on behalf of a young man who died. The match was to be played in four 20minute quarters, with all the lads who had been at training, getting a run out.

The ref got the game underway and within five minutes, a wayward pass was quickly intercepted. The oppositions' winger, wasted no time in steaming across the try line. I thought, five minutes gone and we've been split apart already. The next ten minutes, was crash, bang and wallop, then,after a slick move, if I say so myself, the Yardley try line was breached.

Here we were, the real life mean machine, battling with an established rugby club and drawing.

Yardley stepped up the pace and after a break down in communication, our line was broken again. We battled away for the remainder of the quarter, showing the heart of warriors on a battle field. Then with the first twenty minutes up, the whistle went. The expected slaughter, was not materialising and as far as we were concerned, the upset was still a reality.

The second quarter saw the introduction of a few new players. The main one being, Andy Jonah lomu. Yardley were now on the back foot and I could see the tension amongst their supporters.

It was now one way traffic and when the ball eventually got to Andy, a try was inevitable. Andy, as he had done in practice, skipped past one challenge and skilfully evaded another. With a blistering burst of speed, he sailed between the rugby posts. It was two try's each and with the second quarter drawing to a close, we knew Yardley would go to plan B.

Plan B,was obvious to all of us and that was, get some first team players out. The third quarter was very much one way traffic, with Yardley running in two quick try's. The fact they needed to call on the first team players, highlighted the pressure they were under. To us, this was a clear sign of panic.

The last quarter, was greeted with a sudden down pour. This gave the spectators, a good excuse to run to the bar. Anyway, the match resumed and we battled away again. We were throwing our bodies, in front of everything that moved and giving as good as we got.

The referee shouted 'final attack' and after a frantic bit of ball passing, the whistle was finally blown. We proceeded to shake hands and gave each other the 'hip hip hoorays'. Hand shakes and laughs were exchanged and we all left the field, proud of our performance. We may not of won the match, but we gave them a mighty scare and that alone,was worth it.

GOOD & BAD DOOR MEN

Most of the situations I refer to, are based on my time, working at a bar called the Pit Stop. This particular bar, was situated in James Brindley place,which is found in Birmingham. I will share numerous scenes, that all doormen will immediately relate to. I will also discuss, the dangerous ways, in which we are expected to deal with them.

At no time at all,do I want to come across, as an expert in any particular field of security. I firmly believe however, some of the situations we're confronted with, can be dealt with, by the use of coming sense.

The ten metre walk, is based on how you deal with certain situations, form the point of seeing it, A, to confronting it, B.

Also, the various thoughts and emotions, that are experienced. These feelings,can be both positive and negative.

I remember an evening,where five or six stocky lads, starting misbehaving in the bar. I knew it was only a matter of time, before a confrontation would take place. The confrontation, could only go two ways, very good, or very bad.

I approached the lads and told them to tone it down. They gladly did, for approximately two seconds. I stood by the door and smiled. Here we go again. How often do we find ourselves, in these predictable situations. Punters taking things to far and not leaving you any choice, but to act.

I told the other two doormen the situation, and mentally got ready to sort it. As I began walking towards these guys, it seemed to all come together. I'd been in this situation a hundred times and operated on automatic pilot. For some reason, the simplicity of it all, was never as clear as now.

If during the ten metre walk,you allow the negative thoughts, at point A, to out way the positives at point B, you've already lost. Before the very first step is taken,you could be facing catastrophe. I mentioned previously, I had good lads around me, during the naughty days. Having decent chaps around me, made some situations easier to deal with.

The door game in this day and age,is far from easy. With the promotion of cheap drinks and peoples desire to drink themselves senseless, its far from easy. The threat of a drunken punter,is never far away and for whatever reason, pubs, are cutting down on security. I can only imagine, there is a financial reason for doing this. The safety of the punters, within a pub or a club, should be the ultimate priority. Why doormen are being given near impossible tasks, is very troubling.

I have confronted a few managers, about the running or their establishments and received a poor response. After sifting through the ambiguous answers, I am often left disappointed. Its fairly obvious really, turn over at the tills,is the number one priority.

But what can we do? After all, were only the doormen. Whose job is obviously easy. Wake up bar managers, and please listen, its not easy. To monitor the hot spots, the door, the exits and keep the peace,is not easy. We are also called upon, to administer first aid and of course, eject the drunkards.

With all these obstacles and odds stacked against you, priority number one my friend, is safety. Make sure you're working with a good team of staff. You'll find, when you have an established team, its worth its weight in gold.

As previously mentioned. During the time of the football violence, it's better to have ten good men beside you, than thirty bad ones. When working with decent door staff, some of the most awkward situations, can be made a lot easier.

It was a typical Thursday night at the Pit Stop. A group of lads had arrived about eight pm and hell bent on trouble. At about eight thirty pm, one of the regulars Christopher, told me he was far from happy. The lads mentioned, were starting to perform.

Apparently, they were throwing drinks over themselves, almost drenching Christopher's girlfriend in the process. I took this on board and saw where they were drinking. I approached them, in a firm but friendly manner. "Come on lads you're here to have a good time, don't spoil it" I said.

This was a typical Pit Stop setting. Lads were huddled together, laughing, shouting and being as loud as they could.

Anyway, as time passed, instead of getting better, they got worse. They were drinking at break neck speed and getting louder and louder. My little chat, obviously had little influence and I knew the punters weren't happy.

I looked across at the group of lads. There they were, giving themselves and whoever was in range, non stop Budweiser baths. I had seen enough. There were three of us on this night. A doorman from the bar upstairs, a decent guy called Kirk, had come for a chat. This now meant,we were effectively four.

I said to Reuben,who was one of the team, these lads have outstayed their welcome, they have to go. Every one nodded, we were one. "You've had enough lads, its time to go" I said. This was met with the usual "come on mate were really sorry, give us a break".

They numbered about seven, so we stood in a manner, where all angles were covered. I made it my priority, to watch for any surprises. "You're going now" I said, leaving no room for drunkard banter.

I moved my arm behind one lad, the other doormen followed suit. At the sight of us all moving together in unison, the lads put up little resistance. The fact we all moved together, with the same objective, made us a stronger force. It also reinforced the fact,we weren't messing.

The boss Pete said "take them out the side door", I said to him, blokes like this, need to go through the front. The reason for this was simple, they had come in with an arrogant attitude and upset the whole pub. I wanted them to know, they were being taken out on our terms and the whole pub was going to see it.

This serves two purposes, firstly, it shows the punters in the bar, you're in control. Secondly, it discourages any other potential troublemakers, from thinking they can also play up.

When I was a lad in my twenties, my pals and I from the football, were always in trouble. We would always be involved, in some issue or the other. The constant clashes, with the local doormen, were commonplace. Some we actually grew to respect, while others, we had no time for.

Coming from a football background, most of the local doormen knew, we could get a serious fighting force together; at the click of a finger. They knew, that without much effort at all; we could have a mini army outside their door.

I always remember a doorman called Neil, he was well and truly one of the old school. When most clubs closed the door, Neil would welcome us in. Neil would let us know, he was taking a risk, "don't let me down lads". Was his famous catchphrase.

I liked Neil and within reason, he was never let down. We respected him. As fate would have it, Neil ended up working on the same door as me. Neil didn't half remind me, of the bother I used to give him. I could only laugh and shake my head. Neil knew, at the end of the day, he was always regarded with the utmost respect.

Men like Neil, fill other doormen with confidence. The minute he mentioned, he was working with me, I knew he was a man, I could totally rely on. I remember having conversations with Neil, about the way things have changed. We would talk about this generation and what were up against.

Ten to fifteen years ago, a fight wouldn't be solved, by the producing of an automatic. The threat of a comeback would always be there, but the immediate threat of being blown away, wouldn't.

The way the door game as gone today, staff have to ask their pals, to come down to the pub. There's nothing wrong with that at all, especially if your expecting trouble, but its still worrying.

I've also noticed, more and more lads are saying to me, "Joe Blogs as got no courage, I may as well be on the door by myself" I'm also hearing people say "so and so, never backed up so and so last week". Hearing all these murmurings, worries me.

If a person genuinely believes, he's working with suspect lads, then move on. The game your in, is far,far, to dangerous. Second guessing, a next man's ability, can be extremely fatal.

If your feelings are accurate and Joe Blogs does turns out to be suspect, then you'll have chosen wisely. My final comment, in regards to this matter, is this; if and when their eventually found, be extremely relieved.

I read an article, about a German nightclub owner and the methods he was employing to quell trouble. His secret, was to employ nude door staff, the article was headed, Naked bouncers, reduce violence.

The article.

A German nightclub says, it as doubled its turnover and reduced the level of violence, after it started using naked women as bouncers.

Management Beat club in Cologne, came up with the idea as a way to combat trouble makers. Club goer Stefan Wurz said "it makes standing in the queue,a lot more fun". "When they come out on the streets,they have to wear a coat, but it's not fastened and there's plenty to see. It takes your mind off everything else."

Linda 26, says the job is a lot easier and more fun than being a lap dancer, which was her previous occupation. She said "you get to meet people and I haven't had any trouble at all". "If they are over 18 and well dressed, they have a good job of getting past me."

Beat club boss Philippe Sommer, 26 said "with our new bouncers we wanted to tone down the atmosphere of aggression that often exists". He added that, the idea had also boosted visitor numbers and added; "It makes the visit to our club, all the more enjoyable."

THE BAD

When I talk about the ten meter walk, it may appear, it basically consists of bravery and brawn. If this seems to be the case, then I've erred greatly from my objective.

During that ten meter walk, we can take on a mind set, that is steadfast and also flexible. Many punters come up to me and I hazard a guess you, and say, 'your alright, but that other ones moody, why cant he be like you?'.

Normally I smile and say he's alright and that's the end of that. What punters fail to see is, were all individuals, who deal with situations and people differently. Not every one shows their pearly whites,every two minutes and the fact is, some would see it as weakness.

I find, when there's a need to smile, you smile. Why for the sake of punters, should you walk around, like the proverbial Cheshire cat. Some doorman, adopt the stern face approach, others have the smiling face. Whatever category you come into, as long as the jobs done right, that's all that matters.

Don't be unduly distracted, by petty things. If you're doing the job well, then stick to your style.

Being courteous however,costs nothing and can often go a long way. This I feel, is the natural way for an individual to act. Treat people, in the same manner, you expect to be treated. More often than not, if this behaviour is applied,you'll see the benefits.

Some doormen,unfortunately go to far,during the course of their work. The fact is, in every walk of life, there are good and bad tradesmen. Just like a bad footballer, a bad doorman, stands out a mile.

Years gone by,doormen were somewhat hand picked. A friend would vouch for the credibility of his mate and his role as a bouncer, would begin. This being the case, the chances were, if you were an established door-person in your field; you wouldn't recommend someone lacking guts. The person you vouched for, would have your reputation, in their hands.

We are now entering a time, where the local job centres, advertise for door supervisors. Lets face it, there are some right loose canons out there. When the council agrees a license, to a lunatic, what do you think will happen. The sad thing about the door game is, one or two bad apples, gives the whole grocery a bad name. Believe you me, many doormen have taken a beating, off the back of someone else's bad attitude.

I always adopt the attitude, respect everyone. Whether they are black, white, tall or short, respect them. As the well used saying goes, never judge a book by its cover, unless its blatantly obvious to do so. Unfortunately, there are many, who don't approach this principle and more often than not, get a rude awakening.

Every would be doorman, or a lad looking for a reputation, will encounter trouble. The doorman seeking a tough guy reputation, will be faced with a make or break situation. Which for his reputations sake, will either make him,or break him. We are now well and truly engrossed in a society,rampant with fruit cakes and extremely violent people. Yet through witnessing various incidents, one thing still remains, men seeking violence. Sadly in some cases folks, it's a doorman.

I remember working at the Pit Stop bar, which for some unlucky punters, ran alongside a canal.

One particular doorman at the time, was going through some family issues. The doorman told me what the problems were and how upset he was feeling. I listened intently and gave him whatever sympathy I could. In truth, I didn't know the doorman that well, so I found it very hard, to give any deep advice. Nonetheless,as a colleague, I tried my best.

Anyway, during the course of the night,I was called to the front door. What took place next, was an absolute disgrace. I saw the doorman in question, holding a lad in a headlock. There was another doorman present, but there was no need to get involved.

I always make a point, never be too quick to judge. One thing I can honestly say though, is this. The lad who was being man handled,was the original seven stone weakling. The lad was thrown on the floor and before you could intervene, picked up and thrown into the canal.

I remember looking at another doorman Clive and thinking, what on earth is going on. I said to myself, did that really happen?

The looks of astonishment, on everyone's face, said it all. The punters in the crowd, clearly left you in no doubt, as to what they thought. The overall atmosphere, was one of total disbelief. I had been told before,of numerous punters swimming in the canal, but this was clearly high jinx. This particular occasion however, was totally uncalled for'.

I looked at Clive, he looked at me. I knew we both felt the same. What had just happened,was sickening to all. Clive and I, just shook our heads in total disbelief. I can honestly say, I have never felt so sickened,by this act of excessive force. Though I had no part of it and Clive had no part of it, I felt as if I had done it myself. I honestly felt ashamed, at what I had just witnessed.

When the lad pulled himself out the canal, my heart sank. Seeing this young kid, drenched from head to toe and staggering around all over the place,was pitiful. He was shaking for dear life and looked terrible.

Did the punishment fit the crime ? you might well ask. The answer is No, with a capital N. He had drunkenly said to the doorman "I could have you" Nothing more, nothing less. Simply an empty threat, from a seven stone drunken youth.

"I could have you". Most doormen I know, would have laughed in his face. It would have been the laugh of the night and left at that. The doorman in question however, took it further. In response to the drunken challenge, the lad was excessively handled and thrown into the dirty water.

When my girlfriend picked me up that night, I told her what had happened and just how sick I feel. She said, the fact I feel this bad, shows a decent heart, and doormen like that,don't last very long.

This was small consolation, as being there, made me feel responsible. God knows me, a lot better than I know myself ; and folks, this wasn't my style. Some may be cruel enough to say, he deserved it. If you're one of them, ask yourself this question, what would have happened, if he'd never surfaced. The answer is simple, manslaughter.

I did talk to this doorman, about this incident and he did express regret. "as soon as I threw him Elvis, I thought, what have I done" He went on to say "I don't want people to think, I'm just another bully, I'm not that sort of bloke".

I can whole heart-idly appreciate stress and the way it can make you unpredictable. Its very easy to do some weird things and way out of character. It does seem strange however, that a stressful persons anger, is often taken out, on someone half their size.

Another incident, that took place at the Pit stop, again, had me shaking my head in disbelief. Once again, it was the over the top approach of a colleague.

It was a typical summers evening, punters were flocking through the doors and getting in the party mood. The usual banter took place at the door, "hello mate, how are you, long time no see" etc. The regular doormen comments,were also at the fore. Anyway, as the evening progressed, the barman approached me. He told me, two lads were acting stupid and needed to leave. I asked him where they were and he pointed them out. He went on to say, they had already been barred, but had somehow slipped the net. I gave the doorman the run down and off we went.

I was working with a particular doorman, who I will call D. As we approached these lads, I noticed bottles and pint glasses in close attendance; would be weapons of war, potentially deadly.

D approached the one, I the other. "Your barred lads, its time to go"I said. The lad I was talking to, stepped back. I watched him very closely. I had already checked his hands, they were empty.

He realised arguing his point was fruitless and acknowledged what I said.

There was I, thinking all was well, when all of a sudden bang! D was on top of his mate, exercising his vice type grip. Blood was pumping out the lad's nose. At this point, I said to D "get him up and take him outside". The lad I was dealing with, put up no restraint and with a little helping hand, went straight through the exit door.

Once outside, I considered the little altercation over and the matter sorted. D however, had other ideas. A nose that was already bashed, was bashed some more."Don't ever pull a bottle on me, ill kill you". D had lost the plot. I had to pry his fingers apart, from the lads' nose and literally drag him off. I told D to disappear, what had taken place, was seen by everyone.

To understand just how bad it looked, I will try to paint a clearer picture.A nice summers evening by the canal, people drinking and enjoying the sun. Twenty punters in the queue, another thirty sipping beer outside. Through the exit door, comes a bloodied and beaten man, in the full view of everyone. D continues to give the beaten man,more aggressive treatment. People are cringing at the sight of the blood. To cap it all off, I have to physically stop him. It was a situation,that looked extremely bad, for all concerned. It wasn't pretty by a long way.

I told D to clean himself up and have a story ready for the police. I wasn't happy with what had just happened,but I tried to give D,an heads up. I told D,punters very rarely look favourably on doormen, so expect no glowing references.

Before the words, had time to sink into his head, along came two police officers. They were accompanied,by the bruised and battered lad. D was taken away and I never saw him again.

What had taken place that evening, would not impress most doormen. The fact remains, there's many a loose canon, working the door. D was also the doorman, responsible for throwing weakling into the canal and deep down, I thought him a bully.

DID BOUNCERS DROP HIM ON HIS HEAD?

I read an article from an American newspaper, which was titled; did Bouncers Drop Him on His Head?, it read as follows.

Early January 2002 Jeri Casuccio lay in bed, fretting as to the whereabouts of her husband Guy, a 38 year old gym owner. Figuring he had forgotten his cell phone, Jeri dozed off between midnight and 1am. About the same time, her husband was lying bloodied and disorientated, after being ejected from a club; by bouncers and an off duty policeman.

At 4am, the phone jolted Jeri awake, someone from the local hospital had said there had been a bar fight. Guy had hit his head and was being held for observation. Jeri assumed it was nothing to get too worked up about; She got up, got ready and arranged for a baby sitter to take care of their children.

The hospital was called back, this time she got a very different story. Her husbands injuries were grave, shed better get to Oakland straight away.

Guys chances of survival were 50-50, he was conscious but combative. There was bleeding in his brain, guys night had turned into a nightmare.

That day, Jeri had filed an assault report with police, based on information she got from one of her husbands friends. She told officers, that bouncers from bar Pittsburgh, had roughed up her husband. During guys first week in hospital, doctors removed part of his brain, and inserted a tube in his head to drain fluids. Another operation removed the front portion of his skull, to accommodate swelling of his brain. He sank into a month long coma.

By early April two bouncers had been arrested and an off duty officer, had come under an internal investigation.

Casuccio who had come out his coma, was under going physical therapy and grappling with medical bills; of more than $1 million.

On April 17, the couple filed a lawsuit against Bar Pittsburgh. It alleged negligence and conspiracy by out of control bouncers and police officers moonlighting at the club.

Depending on who's telling the story, Guy had either been attacked by bouncers in an unprovoked assault, or had hit his head, after slipping from the grasp of several bouncers.

At 6ft plus and 250 pounds, Casuccio was a big man, who regularly worked out at his gym. He had set out on that evening, with some of his friends and after stopping of at a couple of bars, had ended up in Bar Pittsburgh.

According to his attorney, a bouncer approached him and asked him to leave, soon their witnesses maintain, other bouncers and a police officer approached Casuccio. Suddenly someone put him in a head lock, his face turned red and he stopped struggling. Some accounts say two people carried him out.

The Casuccio attorney, likens what happened next, to the wrestling move known as the pile driver. After hitting him in the head, knocking him down and kicking him, the court complaint claims, Bar Pittsburgh employees, marched him outside; tilted his head and drove his skull into the concrete.

As Casuccio lay bleeding outside, another patron Curt Smith, lay about 5 feet away. Smith says he was thrashed by bouncers, in an unrelated incident. He ended up with concussion, broken nose and nearly two dozen stitches in his chin; Smith claims, that bouncers dragged him outside by his feet, as his head slammed against the steps.

"I was dancing, the next thing I know, I was in hospital." Smith said "I was unconscious, I was kicked in the head about five times, by one of the bouncers and the only thing I remember, is waking up."

The Casuccios law suit filed in Beaver County Common Pleas Court, asks for at least $25,000 from bar Pittsburgh and its parent company, B, N, Y, Penn Inc.

Another claim, is that bar Pittsburgh bouncers, were making an example of Casuccio; as a warning to anyone else, who might act up. The suit, accuses off duty officers,of conspiring with bouncers and looking the other way during incidents.

There are always two sides to a story, here is the other. The night Guy was injured, a police officer Jason Behun, was moonlighting with other officers at Bar Pittsburgh. Dressed in police uniform, he started at 11.30pm. According to a report he wrote, he was standing outside the bar at 1am and a club employee told him a patron was harassing people and trying to start fights.

Behun entered the bar with bar Pittsburgh staff and watched as they approached the intoxicated male and asked him to leave. The man refused, and refused twice more when Behun asked him to leave. When Behun started to tell the man a third time, the man raised his arm in an aggressive manner. Behun grabbed the arm, two club employees rushed forward, one gripping the other arm and the other grabbing his feet.

The three men, began carrying the man outside. Behun wrote;

"While carrying the suspect out, he continued to actively resist, by thrashing with his arms and legs, as we approached the door, the suspect was still resisting. As I was going through the threshold, my foot slipped from underneath me, on the wet icy sidewalk and I landed on my knee. The staff member holding the suspects arm, also lost his footing and fell to the ground. This caused the suspect to fall to the ground, hitting the back of his head on the sidewalk. The suspect suffered a cut head. I had a bruised knee, a medic was called via the radio.

A large crowd of people had started to gather around, so I began to assist with crowd control. At this time, friends of the suspect, emerged from the bar and fled with the suspect."

Also named as a defendant, was a Christopher Burnett. Burnett was out with Casuccio that night. The suit alleges, that Burnett may have aggravated Casuccios injuries, by carrying him a block and propping him up sides a vehicle, before medics arrived.

Todd Wateska, a 27 year old car salesman, was in Bar Pittsburgh that night. He says he saw a muscular man, wearing a jersey with rolled up sleeves, push a smaller man out of his way. Wateska would later find out, from a homicide detective, that the muscular man, was Guy Casuccio.

"He pushed him out the way like a fly, we all looked at him like, he was an idiot" Wateska said. "You could tell he was antagonistic and looking for trouble." Watseka's friends, alerted the clubs bouncers, and watched as a few of them approached Guy and asked him to leave. Wateska couldn't hear the discussion, but he said he could see Guy smirking and shaking his head.

More bouncers arrived, along with a uniformed officer. Guy's friends were also there, "one took off his shirt, as if to prepare for a scrap" Wateska said. A melee broke out, as the bouncers hustled Casuccio and his friends' away. Wateska didn't see what happened outside. "Everything I saw, happened inside, and he was well deserving of, it" Wateska said. As officer James Goga, interviewed Wateska and other witnesses that night, two females told the officer, that Guy Casuccio, had grabbed their behinds.

At the end of March, police charged two Bar Pittsburgh employees, Kevin Thompson and Robert Murphy, with aggravated assaults, on Casuccio and Smith. A Chief of police, was asked to look at officer Behuns actions.

The attorney for Thompson and Murphy described his client's jobs as "good will ambassadors" and noted the conflicting stories about what happened to Casuccio.

"If I take a patron out, that I think is obnoxious and I slip and drop him, that isn't a criminal act," the attorney said. "Further more, we have the evidence of a police officer; do we have any reason to believe Behuns lying? I don't think so."

CASUCCIO, THE VERDICT

Thursday July 18 2002

One of the former employees, of the bar Pittsburgh club, will face criminal charges. During a preliminary hearing, Chief Magistrate William Simmons, dismissed aggravated assault and reckless endangerment, against Thompson, 23.

Thompson was accused of beating Guy Casuccio, 38 and Curt Smith on January 20 at Bar Pittsburgh. Both men were hospitalised, Casuccio with severe brain and head injuries.

The district attorneys office, dropped charges against David Catalano 35, a second former employee of bar Pittsburgh. In both cases, there were problems finding eye witnesses, who could identify the accused men. Simmons, held for trial, the third man accused in the beating; Robert Murphy 23. He also faces charges of aggravated assault and reckless endangerment.

"If my attorneys happy, I'm happy" Casuccio said after the two hour hearing.

Bar Pittsburgh still faces civil litigation in Casuccio' case. The night club, voluntarily closed in May, following discussions with district attorney Stephen Zappala Jr; who was concerned that the business was becoming a nuisance.

When I first read this article, I read it with an open mind. I didn't want to favour one side (bouncer) or the other side (punter).

Whatever conclusions I have reached, are based on the limited evidence before me.

From the information and eye witness testimonies, it would appear,Guy wasn't blame free. When we look at him physically, what we see is a man over 6ft plus and over 250lbs (18 stone). Basically,we have a powerful man, who ran is own gym. To the average punter in a bar, a very intimidating site.

If we disregard the fact the bloke was big, which by itself is no reason to throw him out, it would appear, his general behaviour caused the confrontation. He had been to a couple of bars previously, so there's every possibility he was a little tipsy. I would imagine, a few more drinks would be downed in the night club. This would more than likely,make him even more tipsier. Just an opinion

One punter in the club claimed, Guy brushed aside a small man and was walking around the club in an obnoxious manner. When confronted, it is alleged one of Guys pals, took his shirt off, ready for the impeding punch up. There was also the accusation of grabbing women's behinds. There are always,two sides to a story. Based on this particular side, it would seem the bouncers had little option,but to eject him.

The bottom line is this. Something got drastically out of hand,but thank God, no one died. The events after the ejection, are separate issues and I wouldn't even try to comment about them. The verdict given,was not guilty. Quoting Guy Casuccio "If my attorneys happy I'm happy"

At least Guy still as his life. I was contacted buy Guy, via the internet. Guy explained his side of the events. I told Guy, I don't sit in judgment of anyone and only read what is placed before me. I got the impression,Guy was now a God fearing man, and if this is the case, praise God.

A lot of doormen, treat the black suit and bow tie, as a shield of invincibility. It reminds me of a cartoon,or a kids super hero. In the day time, Tom is just an ordinary post man, but at night, he becomes Bouncer Man, the most fearless super hero of them all.

What we should realise is, no matter how good we look, we are only human beings. No matter, how powerful the suit makes us feel, at the end of the day,were just ordinary blokes. We are just folks earning extra cash, trying to make things a little bit easier. You should never let the job overwhelm you,or go to your head. The job can be very cruel,so don't use it, to inflate your flagging ego.

I remember a lad in school, called Dicken. He was the kind of lad,who always wore trendy clothes and the latest fashion trainers.

He would always desire, the reputation of a feared tough guy. He would constantly talk about, the tough associates of his Dad.

Before we left school,his conversations, were all about drinking beer and fighting.

I knew by the way he talked, he wanted to be regarded as a tough guy. Sadly for him however, no one took him seriously.

Some three or four years, after leaving school, a market trader called Jason, stopped me. "Remember that Dicken form school Elvis, he reckons he punched you, outside his pub."I laughed out loudly.

This was the firs time, I heard his name, since leaving school. I carried on with my day to day activities, laughing to myself. It transpired, that he had left school and entered the world of bouncing. He was now touting himself, as a bit of a tough guy.

"Punched me outside his pub, I must have a twin brother", I said to myself. I hadn't laid eyes on him, since the day I left school. Why on earth,would a man feel the need to lie like that. The mans ego and self esteem, were obviously very low in deed.

Why he needed to conjure up stories like this,were beyond me. It didn't take me long to figure out, his new role as a bouncer, had given him, a false sense of bravery. The opportunity to establish himself and flex some muscle, was now his desire.

I laughed it off and dismissed him instantly from my thoughts. After having a chat with another friend,who also told me, Dicken, was bad mouthing me, I knew something had to be done. He was now well and truly, in a part of the world, he longed for. With a bit of investigation, I found out where he was working. Dicken was now plying his trade, at the Grapes public house, in Birmingham city centre.

I went to the Grapes pub, but he wasn't there. I went to a few more supposed sites and he wasn't there either. I thought forget this, we'll meet sooner, or later.

A short time after this, I saw another friend called Mark and we got talking."Do you ever see Dicken?" I asked "no one sees him Elvis" was the reply "Why, as he immigrated" ? I asked. The answer I received,was straight to the point. "No Elvis, he's dead"

I couldn't believe my ears, how ironic, Dicken was dead. It was said at the time, he was in a pub in Coventry and an argument between a couple broke out. Apparently, he got involved and tried to throw his weight around. This was met with a bottle to his head, which left him vomiting. He was taken to a local hospital and later died.

Life is just so unpredictable and we can't guarantee, the way things will turn out. I do believe however, certain choices and decisions we make, go a very long way; in creating the situations we end up in.

Working the door, can be an introduction to a world of violence. For those who feel they've lead a somewhat sheltered life, it as an attractive appeal. Working the doors, opens up a lot of avenues and offers.

From initially bouncing, you can move on to debt collecting, car clamping and minding. You can also find yourself, being employed as a paid bully, or amateur hit man. The avenues are endless. Unfortunately, when you least expect it, the glamour can quickly disappear. When the reality of violence hits home, it can be life changing.

I was asked by a good friend, to work at a pub called the Astbury Tavern. This particular pub, was on the outskirts of Birmingham. My friend Claude, gave me the run down of what to expect. Claude also filled me in on the general history of the pub. He told me of a story, which I sadly hear, far too often. This of course, was of the super doorman. The man who's worked all the rough pubs, and basically walks through walls, for fun.

The story went as follows;

Claude was working along side a lad called G and a new chap from Blackpool. The chap from Blackpool, had an awful lot to say. Apparently, he claimed to work the roughest and toughest bars around the town. With all the introductions over, the lads went to their allotted positions and began working.

It was a typical busy night, the punters were drunk and doing the things punters do. An incident broke out with a group of lads, which turned out far from pretty.

A girl,who was associated with the lads, pulled a knife on the boss Steve. This never went down well and consequently, the group ended up outside.

The night progressed, without further incident and the punters left and went on there merry way. Claude and the lads relaxed and with pints in hand, sat down to an end of night beer.

Through the windows of the pub, a group totaling about fourteen, began shouting racial abuse. The disgruntled group, were quickly recognised. The troublesome crowd, from the incident before,were back again. It was clear to all concerned,they were looking for round two.

Unfortunately for the door staff involved, the cold beers, would have to wait. A decision had to be made. The choices were simple, phone the police, or deal with it themselves. Claude and G said "lets deal with it" The doormen from Blackpool,chose otherwise.

Claude and G, went outside and the fighting erupted. Two doormen,vastly outnumbered. Coshes, bottles, and battle cries, were at the heart of the fight. The mob expected an easy fight and something of a walkover. Well, they were certainly right, they got walked right over. Two of them needing hospital treatment.

An argument could be made, that the police should have been immediately called. I can't dismiss this argument, but something needs to be explained. In this particular case, the right thing, from a doorman's point of view,could turn out to be wrong thing.

The Astbury tavern, is a dream come true, for those who enjoy, breaking windows. The pub, must have at least, forty large panes of glass, just crying out to be smashed. If a disgruntled group, decided to come back for trouble, it could get very messy in deed. They could quite easily, shower the unsuspecting punters,with glass.

After working there, I could see why Claude and G took the fight out side. If they waited for the police to arrive, there could quite easily be, carnage. Not only that, the area, is very tight knit. Any disturbance, involving locals beating up doormen,would have circulated in an instant. The fact the tables were turned, makes this altercation, a very sore point.

Fortunately, the injuries to Claude and G,were very minor. It was a situation, where they both went for it. At the end of the day, they got away relatively unscathed. For that alone gentlemen, give God thanks.

When Claude told me the story, I smiled to myself. The doorman from Blackpool,who claimed to be as hard nails, wanted no part in any fighting. It would of been interesting, if this Blackpool doorman, was needed to stop an in house disturbance. My only comments are these, be extremely grateful, you managed to cope with the situation and no one was badly hurt.

THE BAD CHRISTMAS SPIRIT

While working at a pub, during the dreaded Christmas period, I noticed a lad with a pint in one hand and half a pint in the other. Unsurprisingly, he looked worse for wear. I watched him stagger around and could see he was on the brink of falling. This was the typical office boy, whose sole objective, was to get wrecked with his mates.

To lose himself in the Christmas spirit, was his number one priority. I watched him stagger and sway through the crowd, so I decide to have a word. The last thing I wanted to see, was somebody spilling beer everywhere. I was about to approach him, but was called to attend something else. I dealt with the distraction and then went about finding him. Unfortunately, he had disappeared.

I took up my position by the exit door and observed the punters. I spotted office boy, staggering towards me, he looked terrible. He stumbled right beside me and slumped against the door. Normally, if someone gets themselves into that sort of a state, they are asked to leave. I looked at the time, it was ten forty pm. We would be shutting in twenty minutes, so I gave him some leeway. "Find a seat with your pals, if not, you have to go" I said.

This was met with a blunt "no! I'm standing here, I don't want to sit down". What this chap failed to see was, I was giving him the opportunity, to stay. The way in which he was answering me, was bringing him closer and closer to an ejection.

I gave him a simple choice, either sit down, or get ready to be ejected. He reluctantly sat down. I was extending a bit of Christmas Spirit and it was being thrown straight back at me.

Office boy, took a seat right next to me. He was clearly angry and started making a point, of staring at me. I could hear his pals, telling him to behave himself. Unfortunately, office boy, was having none of it.

I glanced in his direction and again, he stared back at me. Only now, he began cursing under his breath. It was at this point, my Christmas spirit ran out. If a bloke wants to stare at me and curse me to my face, what will he do, if my backs turned.

I took the pint glass out his hand and ushered him through the exit doors. Office boy, fell into some tables outside and lay on the floor, gazing into space. A couple of his pals, who had seen what had happened, told him to get up. They told him, it served him right. Some on the other hand, weren't too pleased.

The doormen I was working with, laughed when they saw him. He was sitting on his backside and mumbling to himself. Office boy, wasn't the biggest of blokes, but as they say, don't judge a book by its cover.

I did see the funny side and laughed about it afterwords. This was just one of those silly Incidents. You could easily be looked upon as being a bully, because the punter you're dealing with, is a small framed chap. If office boy,was six foot four and seventeen stone, it would be seen,as a job well done. On this occasion however, office boy wasn't and life goes on.

In defense of doormen, I find that no one ever gives the doormen, the benefit of the doubt. If your dealing with a punter, built like a gorilla, no one as much to say. As far as everyone's concerned, you're doing your job. However, if you forcibly eject a small bloke, you're seen as a bully, throwing their weight around.

To the naked eye, a big bloke being ejected, is more acceptable than a small bloke being ejected. What most people fail to realise is, a small bloke, is often just as aggressive as a big one. Given half a chance,they wouldn't think twice about smashing a bottle over your head.

Due to the reputations of some doormen, you just can't win. I find the best judge of a doorman, is another level headed doorman.

I was talking too a doorman, called Wassim and a few of the lads,who work at the Lloyds bar in Broad St. I asked how the New Years

Eve celebrations went, and the look I received, basically said it all. The Lloyds bar, was a battle zone, and the night would be long remembered.

As the bell rang at midnight, the "Happy New Years" were said, and as the clock struck ten past twelve; they were well and truly forgotten.

Wassim and the lads, went on to tell me what took place, and believe you me, I didn't envy them. There were thirty lads going hammer and tongs upstairs, while another war, was taking place down stairs. It was all hands on deck, icebergs everywhere.

The first incident, involved a group of lads;who made a point of starting trouble, with some black and an Asian guys. This resulted, in a punch up on the dance floor. Punches and kicks, reigning down from all angles. The end result was, bodies being ejected, through the main doors. The same lads, had given a black bar man some racial abuse. Sadly, it doesn't take rocket science; to work out the type of people they were.

With one incident dealt with, the spirit of violence, began to circulate. Those with a brain resisted, but those out for trouble, embraced it. The worse nightmares of the door team, were soon to be realised. Mass brawls everywhere, with a handful of staff, to deal with it.

When the first incident took place, the doormen were separated. Once regrouped, they dealt with the problem with ease.

When the second and most violent incident took place, regrouping became very difficult, to say the least.

Wassim told me, the mass brawl upstairs, was started by a woman. For whatever reason, she was trying to glass another woman. The upset woman, wasn't a pupil of Phil Taylor and her thrown glass, missed the target. The glass, ended up smashing into the head, of an innocent bloke. Understandably, this never went down to well and a heated argument took place.

Without stating the obvious, one thing led to another. The end result, being a mass brawl. The fighting involved,well over thirty people. The doormen who were present, were in no position to stop all the fighting, but they tried none the less.

The picture, the doormen painted to me, was far from pretty. It was only after they regrouped,could they perform as a unit. Things were that bad, as they were getting involved upstairs, the SOS came, to break up fighting downstairs.

The bar had become, a wild west saloon. Bottles were being smashed and pint glasses were being thrown. Some people headed for cover, while those who could dodge, headed for the door.

If ever you needed a good team around you, now was the time. This was a scenario, that most doormen fear and hope they never encounter. For those who questioned themselves, the moment of truth, was now here.

The doormen did all they could to protect themselves. Wassim took a few to the ribs, and another doorman, took a couple to the head. Another doorman said "I was trying to get up the stairs and was confronted, by two mad men".

This resulted, in the doorman, having to fight the two of them. Thankfully,none of the door staff were badly hurt. After doing all they could, to stop the mayhem, it was now time for the riot police to take over. The riot police arrived, with swinging batons in hand. The New Year had started, where the last year had finished. Half an hour earlier, it was " Happy New Year;" that was now a distant memory. How fickle we are.

DANGEROUS LADY

During the late eighties early nineties, came the emergence of Bhangra music. Right alongside this music, came the emergence, of rude, troublesome and out of control, Asian gangs.

It was a Friday afternoon and I was asked to work, at a club called the Humming bird. This was to be a small show,featuring up and coming Asian groups. When I got to the club, I spoke to the promoter and asked him, "who else am I working with". The promoter pointed towards two big black guys. A quick introduction was made and we went to work.

The promoter was both shocked and delighted at the numbers that came through the door. He saw it as a great endorsement, to his promotional skills. I on the other hand, was very concerned in deed.

The crowds were flocking into the club, but not because of any great promotional skills. The reason was clearly obvious in my eyes. The masses of crowds, were coming to the venue,because it was a free event.

Anyway. As the afternoon went into the evening, I could feel the atmosphere changing. At about roughly six o'clock, my fears were sadly realised.

I was standing at the top of the stairs and observing the crowd. People were pushing and shoving and the situation turned nasty. A fight broke out between two rival Asian gangs. The doormen, were nowhere to be seen, so I found myself, well and truly alone.

A gang ran through the main doors, yelling and chanting in their native tongue. Once outside, the whole club seemed to follow them. It was like rats to the pied piper. I told myself, the troubles outside, so let them get on with it. I said to myself, killing each other is their business and nothing to do with me.

So here I was, standing by the main doors, watching the days events unfold before my eyes. Then all of a sudden, without any warning, came the words, "get the bouncer, he stabbed my brother"!

Whats this about then ? I wandered. I cast my mind back, to a brief incident, that had taken place earlier. The incident resulted in a few choice words, but nothing more. I was truly at a loss, as to why he was yelling at me. Why I had suddenly become, public enemy number one,was truly a mystery. I stared towards the crowd. They were staring towards me and baying for my blood. I stared back and waited.

I stood outside on the pavement, literally dumb struck. The double doors, had somehow been locked behind me. There was no safe haven about, so I simply got prepared and waited for war.

"He stabbed my brother, get him". A spaghetti western, type battle cry followed and they came for me.

I was even more confused now. With the prospect of being jumped on, not to appealing, I got my fists ready. I remember throwing a wild right, which missed the target, "calm down, calm down" I said to myself. Then I managed to throw a perfect right cross. I temporarily, had one less to deal with. A high flying side kick, was thrown towards me, which grazed my side. Another wild kick,came towards me, but on this occasion, I caught the offending leg. I returned the compliment, with a well aimed and very powerful, front kick.

Things were now very serious. There was a group of guys I knew, standing close by. Their decision, was crystal clear, brother, you're on your own. What I'm going to tell you next, is not exaggerated whatsoever.

Here I was, fighting a lone battle. Defeat was becoming a harsh reality, which got harsher by the minute. My pride wouldn't allow me to run, so I kept on swinging and praying for a miracle.

The prayers, though said light heartedly, were miraculously received. Out the corner of my eye, I could see someone punching and kicking. Who was this courageous person? An ally at last I thought.

I looked to my left, eagerly ready to join forces, with my new found acquaintance. Believe you me folks, I couldn't believe my eyes. My brother in harms, was actually a young teenage woman. When I saw her, I was in a state of shock and disbelief. Don't get me wrong, she wasn't the most prim and proper looking lady, but she was certainly courageous. I can clearly recall her, jumping around outside the Humming Bird and making her presence felt.

She had a lock knife in hand and more than ready to use it. I stood there, swinging and kicking wildly. Still getting my head around my new found help. By now, I was soaking up more blows than I really appreciated; so I concentrated on staying upright.

I battled away,but knew, It was only matter of time; before a proper beating would come. The sirens sounded and the large crowds eventually dispersed.

Fortunately for me and my new found ally, the police brought an end to the battle. I was taken away by two police officers, in front of masses of shoppers.

I was placed into a car and taken to Steel House lane police station. They questioned me for hours, about what had taken place and the stabbing of a lad outside the club. I told the officer "I have no idea at all". Which in reality, was the truth.

None to impressed with my answers, the officer led me back to my cell. Here I was, sitting on the bench of my pale egg shelled cell and waiting. A number of hours had now passed,then from the cell next door,came a voice, "Aye bouncer, bouncer, is that you" ? I thought for a second, it can't be, can it. I laughed to myself. The young lady with the lock knife, was in the cell next door. The Steel House Lane police, had arrested her as well.

My cell door eventually opened and I was taken out. I walked past the young lady's cell' and looked in. She was sitting on a wooden bench, with her feet up. She was wearing a white police boiler suit. I smiled to myself. The police eventually let me go and said they would be in touch. They never were.

I read an article in the evening mail,the following day. It was in relation to a wounding,outside the Humming Bird nightclub. The article claimed, someone had been charged, with a stabbing. The article never went into much detail, but I obviously knew enough.

A week later, I worked at another Bhangra gig, at a night club called, Pagoda Park. On this occasion, all my Zulu friends, were in full attendance. I made sure my back was covered and there was no chance of me being left on my lonesome. Last weeks performance would not be repeated again, of that I was sure.

The events of the Humming Bird, had left me some what annoyed. The way I was set upon, made me want revenge and deep down, I was looking for guilty faces and pay back.

As expected, a fight broke out in the club and the instigators were thrown out. A couple of my friends took a look outside, to make sure I was OK. I was fine and decided to stay outside for a bit.

The rest of my pals were still inside the club, so I went for a little chat with them. I reassured them all was well and I left them drinking. While I was inside the club, doing my patrols,I noticed some individuals I had ejected. They had some how re-entered the club. These guys, were making a nuisance of themselves and hell bent on trouble. I never had time to deal with them right then, as I had a some more pressing issues.

News had got to me, that there was fighting out side, and some of my friends were involved. I never needed to hear any more and headed straight for the door.

I ran outside and there facing me, were about twenty Asians. My friends were punching away, so I joined the fray. I was attacked with a baseball bat, but managed to block the strike. Thankfully, I was wearing an old fashioned crombie coat. Their very heavy, but extremely thick.

Every where you turned,bottles were smashing and punches were hitting home. The razor sharp broken bottles, were being used as a deadly weapons. Pint glasses flew through the air,with deadly accuracy.

A large dust bin was thrown, crashing into a group of lads, like skittles. My friends who were involved in the mayhem, treated it, as just another punch up. To me however, it was the first steps to payback. The Humming Bird incident,certainly wasn't forgotten.

By now, the word had spread to all our friends,who were still inside the club. Some were actually unaware, of what was going on outside. A large fight,was now taking place.

The lads we were fighting, realised they'd bitten off more than they could chew ;and ran for their cars. Datsuns and Toyotas, roared off in all directions. I remember one lad, jumping into a Ford Capri and mounting the curb. The car was now being used as a weapon. The Asian chap, who lived on my road incidentally, was trying his utmost,to run us over. A few well aimed bottles of beer, put pay to that stunt. The driver soon realised, the Ford Capri, wasn't designed for warfare.

When I eventually got back into the club, the doormen were briefed about the history. I told them about last weeks attack, at the Humming Bird. They weren't to pleased and told me, I wasn't insured outside the premises. They let rip, and made it perfectly clear and in no uncertain terms; if I had got hurt, I wouldn't be covered.

The doormen were a good bunch of lads and what they said, was perfectly true. At the time however, I was still learning the ropes. I know what I did was unprofessional, but at the time, it seemed right. I was a twenty two year old, inner city lad, who was brought up in an area; where we looked after our own. At the end of the day folks, I felt a responsibility towards my friends,who were always their for me.

TEN METRE WALK IN EVERY DAY LIFE

T he ten metre walk, can be applied to most situations we face. Especially those involving our every day lives. We all encounter situations, where decisions have to be made i.e. work, family, health, relationships, finance etc.

The decisions we have to make,can often be very good,or sadly very bad. It is often the emotional response we encounter, that makes decision making,very difficult.

From my own experience, when you're involved in a difficult relationship, decision making, can be very difficult. Pressure plays a large part and often makes things very difficult. Doing the so called right thing, can often turn out wrong.

You're not only encountered with emotional turmoil, but also an upset partner. You also begin to worry and start to threat, about the immediate effect on the family. I am trying to explain an issue, which isn't always that straight forward to deal with.

More often than not, at some point during the relationship, a tough decision should have been made. The opportunity to make the ten metre walk was there, but the mind set unfortunately wasn't.

There are lots of couples, in extremely abusive marriages. They desperately want to escape and somehow start afresh. They deeply regret, having ever entered the relationship. Unfortunately folks, that is life, but don't make it a life sentence.

I honestly believe, a lot of people reading this book; know where I'm coming from. The courage to tackle frightening men, comes without hesitation. Dealing with danger, isn't a frightening issue and is often taken in your stride.

However, to say something, that you know will emotionally hurt,can be very daunting. You'd rather fight the giant, than upset the Mrs. When I hear stories of the jilted spouse,they always seem very similar. The comments normally go something like this.

"They should have dealt with their issues,before it came to this"

Personally, I see this as a break down in communication. Normally brought about, by one person feeling overwhelmingly pressured. This sadly, is to the point where, pulling out seems impossible. When sadly the big day comes, the safest option is to run and disappear. Not the best way to deal with things, but I judge you not. Imagine however, what could have been avoided; if the courage was there before hand.

My marriage may not have worked out, but the children have a wonderfully devoted mother. Who without question, would do anything to please them; and for that alone, she deserves the utmost respect.

IN AN UNREWARDING JOB

Nowadays, how often do we hear people complaining about their job. 'I have to go to work tomorrow, my jobs proper awful. I hate it'.
If you were talking to me over the last few years, I would have been one of them. I have been a labourer, tie sales man and metal worker. My employment also includes, painter and decorator, railway worker and bus driver. I don't want to bore you anymore, so I,ll leave it there.

At some point or the other, I enjoyed the camaraderie that you shared with your work mates; but on a whole, I wasn't content.

The job that I most detested, was the bus driving. You held peoples lives in your hand, but were treated poorly. I had considered leaving for about three years, but with children to consider, I stayed. The thought of not providing, was never entertained.

The last year as a West Midlands Travel bus driver, was simply unbearable. I was continuously off sick,for any and every reason. The job had become my number one enemy and I detested it.

My passion, was always sport and fitness. My longing desire, was to be involved in an area, that could help people. I was always a fit person and wanted to achieve various physical goals.

I remember sitting in my arm chair and weighing things up.

I was in a full time job, that pleased everyone but myself. If the trend continued; I would basically be a boy, in an adults body. My life would simply trundle along,pleasing everybody, but myself.

I had become, a please people person and I knew it had to stop. I shook my head, if this scenario continued, I would end up a forty five year old man; full of ifs,buts and only. I would be known as the bus driver for the rest of my life and no disrespect to bus drivers; it wasn't what I wanted. My main concern, was trying to provide regularly for the children; but in bettering myself, I would be benefiting them.

The children would be fine, children often are. I thought about an income and then assured myself, money would come. If things got really bad, I'd go back on the doors. Decision time had come.

During February 2002,a decision was made. I sat down with my union rep, and said "Roger, you won't be seeing me again, it's adios amigo", and I was gone. I never handed him a resignation; all the disciplinary procedures were held in my absence.

I know the decision was the right one and I thank God, I made it. Within a few months of leaving the buses, I went back to the door work. I also enrolled on a personal trainer's course and started writing this book. I know for a fact, if I was still stuck behind the wheel of a bus, none of this would have been possible. What I did, didn't involve a physical ten metre walk; but the decision I had to make,was just as daunting. The decision, was the right one for me; and a decision, I have never, ever regretted. I have highlighted some decisions, that have proved very beneficial for me. The greatest decision however, is found at the end of this book.

RESPECT TO P

I t was roughly 1995 and I had just finished work and decided to have a quick drink in the local pub. The first thing I noticed, was four of the lads, huddled around a table. They were in deep conversation and It was obvious, something was up. They all had stern and serious expressions and were engaged in criminal conversation.

"What's the score then lads?" The answer I received, was fast and to the point, "were robbing a designer shop and now that you're here".

Here we go I thought, as I knew what was coming next. They continued in discussion and then put it to me "we could do with the extra man".

I asked a few more questions and it became clearly evident, something was being overlooked. The car that was being used for the robbery, belonged to one of the chaps. I shook my head. One thing you should never do; is use your own car for any illegal activity. Especially activity, such as this. So here I was, I had gone from operating a press machine, to drinking a pint of Guinness; and now, contemplating a robbery.

A few more details were dealt with; all that remained, was my answer. "Elvis, are you in, or out"? The chaps sat staring at me in silence, while I sat staring back at them. A voice broke the silence "We've been talking about this all day, if you feel unsure Elvis, it's no big deal".

I laughed to myself, then shook my head. The unpredictability of life; I sipped my Guinness and smiled. The pub doors swung open and the chaps were gone.

T was the driver, so he stayed behind the wheel of the car, C, B and P, headed for the shop. To get to this shop, you had to go through an alleyway of other shops; and it emerged in front of you. C had said to the chaps "the minute we get in the shop, nothing stops us".

There they were, heading towards a top designer shop; they got to the alley way and headed for the clothes. Within the next ten seconds, they would be going through the shop door; and helping themselves, to three grand plus,worth of clothes.

P waited by the door, C and B, started filling up the bin liners with clothes.

The manager and the security staff,stood bewildered. They were powerless, to this blatant show of disregard and total disrespect. With bags full to bursting, they headed for the door. To their amazement, the manager started showing signs of bravery; this was quickly halted, with the production of a hammer.

With clothes in bags and robbery seemingly done, they made their get away. P and C, were relatively fit; B on the other hand, wasn't. He was struggling to keep up and had to rely on adrenalin, to keep his legs going.

They got to the car, and after B had finished vomiting, they started filling the boot. Job done they thought. As they say, it isn't over till the fat lady sings; and the fat lady was fast asleep.

They all sat in the car, waiting for T to get it started. With adrenalin racing through their body, they waited. T turned the key, and just like in the movies, the car wouldn't start. T tried again, but a loud rattling noise, was the cars favourite tune. T jumped out the car and tried to push it single hand-idly, no good. The choice was now crystal clear, abandon ship and scarper.

The mistake of using his unreliable car, was now coming back to haunt P. It had now got to the stage, where P was told to leave the car where it was; he decided otherwise. Now was not the time for debate, they all knew what had to be done; and that was get out the area, asap. Everyone headed off in different directions. P on the other hand, remained with his car. One by one, they made their way back to the pub, T, B and C,waited for P to arrive.

Five o'clock became six, six o'clock became seven and seven o'clock; became the worse scenario, P was arrested.

We later found out, P had got the car started and driven off. A police car had been given the necessary information and started to follow him. P had got out the area and after ten to fifteen minutes of observation, was pulled over. With three grand worth of clothes in his boot, he was as guilty as he could be.

Let me explain a little about P. As I walked into the pub that evening, he was the last person I would expect to be involved. P was definitely one of the lads, but unlike the rest of us; he was never in trouble before. If my memory serves me right, he was training to be an accountant and this was his first offence.

P was taken to the police station and questioned about the robbery; he held it together well and never caved in.

I explained earlier in this book, about my ten metre walk theory. How within that walk, the mind set you adopt, can make all the difference. The mind set adopted can give you the necessary edge, when dealing with certain situations.

I can imagine P in his cell, with eyes shut; thoughts of no, no, no, in his head. I know the police were offering him deals; and various avenues of escape. "Give us their names P, don't take the wrap by yourself,". Along with "Come on P, help us and well help you" and all the regular police sweeteners.

I can picture P, taking a deep breath and leaving his cell. This is Point A, entering the interview room Point B, with his mind made up. P would be well and truly focused on what lay ahead.

"I'm giving no names, so do what you want; nothing you say, can change my mind". "As far as I'm concerned, you've got me and that's all you're getting".For the officers Interviewing P,they would have to settle with what they had. P was sent to the crown court and given a custodial sentence.

QUADRANT PARK LETS HAVE IT!

Quadrant Park, **was a nightclub in Liverpool during the early 1990s. It was very well-known in the area and managed to attract a few famous guest DJS. The main styles of music played were acid house and rave. The nightclub was located on Derby Road in Bootle, north of the city of Liverpool, in a converted warehouse. Originally opened in the late 1980s as a snooker hall and mainstream nightclub, there was also a market in the downstairs warehouse area, and the upstairs contained a small social club (the *Harlequin Suite*) which could be hired out for social occasions.**

The building was originally an Owen Owen warehouse, which was purchased by steel magnate James Spencer in the late 1980s to convert into a nightclub and snooker hall. A "Heritage Market" was opened shortly after to make use of the large unused lower floor space. After the Sunday market trade had moved to a nearby dock warehouse (Stanley Market), Quadrant Park started holding raves in the then-vacant space. Quadrant Park's main period of activity began in 1990 and survived until December 1991, despite considerable and persistent licensing issues and unfavorable media attention in newspapers.

Mike Knowler was the initial resident DJ, and soon invited DJ partner Andy Carroll to join him. Carroll and Knowler had previously helped bring acid house music to the city of Liverpool, DJ-ing at the *State* nightclub. Guest DJs at Quadrant Park included Laurent Garnier, Derik May Frankie Bones, and Sasha. When the all-nighter opened, John Kelly, James Barton and Gary Jay joined the resident DJ crew. A loop-hole in a Sefton council law enabled Quadrant Park to be the only legal all-night rave in the UK. Some party goers would travel long distances to get to the venue; from London, Glasgow, Birmingham and even as far away as Aberdeen.

With the history of Quadrant Park established, I will introduce some humour to my book.

Here we were, some eighteen lads from Birmingham; more than ready to party. We hired a mini bus, with the sole intention, to rave on into the early hours. I remember being in this sweltering warehouse, with my hands gyrating and reaching for the stars.

I was an old school raver in his element, rave on people, rave on. The night was going as well as can be expected, but as the good book says, in **1st Thessalonians chapter 5 verse 3**,

"When they say peace and safety, sudden
destruction comes upon them".

Or in our case folks, some body would be breaking into the mini bus; and helping themselves to what ever they could. Here we were, dancing away and losing our minds; when one of the lads comes over to us, and says "we've got a problem",

"Whats the problem" I asked. "Some lads have broken into our mini bus and stolen some leather jackets"was the reply. Well well I thought, I knew what was coming next. Steal from our mini bus will you, very silly. I remember thinking, if your wearing one of our leathers, troubles coming. If anyone's wearing leather jackets that look remotely like ours; its good night Vienna.

We went back into Quadrant Park and made an eighteen man line. We started marching through the dancing ravers. If ever the ten metre walk,was done without hesitation, it was now.

"Let's do it" was shouted and the stalking began. Everyone knew, it could be a potential riot, but such was our mindset,we just didn't care.

I have to laugh; we were stopping people in the middle of their dancing and scanning their leather jackets. If the jacket wasn't recognised, they'd be told to carry on their dancing. Imagine that, eighteen lads stopping ravers in the middle of the dance track; and giving them the once over. It was madness, shear madness. I have to laugh, we were single minded lads, who simply didn't consider consequences.

Steal from us,wrong move. We scoured every corner Quadrant Park had,but with no joy. We said to each other, "what shall we do now" ? We sat in the mini bus, none too happy; but collectively, decided to leave Liverpool. We headed to Birmingham, shaking our heads as we did. Lucky ravers, rave on.

BURNING BUILDINGS

I spoke to a regular at the Pit Stop, who told me he was a roofer. He told me about a sad incident he was part of. It brought home the fact, courage comes in different sizes. Where courage is concerned, it's not the size of the man, but the size of the heart in the man.

Roofer, was working on a house with some of his lads. The usual roofer banter was taking place, with workmen jokes in abundance. The morning was going smoothly, with nothing out the ordinary happening; unfortunately this was too drastically change.

Without warning, roofer was called by one of his colleagues; who was in a state of despair. Roofer was pointed in the direction of the house next door and quickly realised, something was seriously wrong. The adjacent house, was engulfed in flames; smoke was bellowing from the window and more worryingly, two children were still inside.

Roofer and a colleague entered the house, climbing up ladders and scaffold. Their own personal well being, wasn't an issue and it was simply a case of, saving innocent lives.

Roofer said it was a situation, where logical thought didn't apply. When there are lives at stake, all normality of thinking disappears and human nature takes over.

With the house ablaze and smoke thickening by the minute, everyone had to move fast. A young child was rescued, praise God and taken to the safety of the pavement. Roofer said, the heat was unbearable, but it was the intense smoke, that was causing most concern.

The odds were against them, but they desperately searched the house. A frightened young child remained inside and with the visibility worsening, things were looking bad. To continue the search, could result in greater tragedy; so sadly,a decision had to be made.

The brave lads involved, reluctantly left the burning house; tears streamed from their eyes. The intense smoke, along with the emotion of the event, had taken its toll. There was nothing more they could do; they had shown courage of the highest order and though one child perished; thanks to their bravery, another was saved.

A child had died; roofer and all involved, were cut up and devastated. The fact a human life had been lost, left the unfair feeling of guilt.

I told roofer, what he'd done, was brave beyond belief and although a tragedy had taken place; without his actions, it could have been far worse. In a situation like this, where you've literally risked your life for a stranger,feel proud.

Due to your actions, a life was definitely saved form certain death. Guilt my friend, is the last thing you should be feeling.

When you talk to someone and they share experiences like this, it makes you think. You quickly realise, being a giant, or able to knock out everything in your path, doesn't make you brave. There are many people, walking around today; who are not physically strong. These same people folks, may not be physically strong; but psychologically, they are mental giants; with the hearts to match.

Courage, isn't dealing with a situation; where the outcome favours you. Courage, is dealing with a situation; where the out come, is far from certain.

INTERESTING QUOTES

C ourage is almost a contradiction in terms. It means a strong desire to live, taking the form of a readiness to die.

Chesterton, Gilbert Keith

Only a brave person, is willing to honestly admit, and fearlessly face, what a sincere and logical mind discovers.

Alexandria, Rodan of

You will never do anything in this world without courage. It is the greatest quality of the mind, next to honour.

Allen, James Lane

If the highest aim of a captain were to preserve his ship, he would keep it in port forever.

Aquinas, Saint Thomas

Most people live and die with their music still un-played. They never dare to try.

Ash, Mary Kay

Try everything once except incest and folk dancing.

Beecham, Sir Thomas

It's simply wrong to always order kids to stop that fighting. There are times when one child is simply defending his rights and damned well should be fighting.

Bombeck, Erma Louise

Ten people who speak, make more noise than ten thousand who are silent.

Bonaparte, Napoleon

There are only two forces in the world, the sword and the spirit. In the long run,the sword will always be conquered by the spirit.

Bonaparte, Napoleon

Do not pray for easy lives. Pray to be stronger. Do not pray for tasks equal to your powers. Pray for powers equal to your tasks.

Brookes Phillips

It is a brave act to despise death; but where life is more terrible than death, it is then the truest valour,is to dare to live.

Browne, Sir Thomas

Optimism is the foundation of courage.

Butler, Nicholas Murray

The truly brave are soft of heart and eyes, and feel for what their duty bids them do.

Byron, Lord George Gordon Noel

In the depths of winter I finally learned that within me there lay an invincible summer.

Camus, Albert

The courage we desire and prize, is not the courage to die decently, but to live manfully.

> Carlyle, Thomas

Tell a man he is brave, and you help him to become so.

> Carlyle, Thomas

He who loses wealth loses much; he who loses a friend loses more; but he that loses his courage loses all.

> Cervantes, Miguel de

The paradox of courage, is that a man must be a little careless of his life, in order to keep it.

> Chesterton, Gilbert Keith

Taking risks gives me energy.

> Chiat, Jay

Without courage, all other virtues lose their meaning.

> Churchill, Sir Winston Leonard Spencer

Courage is what it takes to stand up and speak; courage is also what it takes to sit down and listen.

> Churchill, Sir Winston Leonard Spencer

Courage is rightly esteemed the first of human qualities, because it is the quality that guarantees all others.

> Churchill, Sir Winston Leonard Spencer

Courage

When I think about courage,I immediately think about, Christian martyrs. History is full of these brave characters, but I will only mention two.

I will begin,with the apostle Steven. The apostle Steven, is often considered, one of the first Christian martyrs. Steven, was stoned to death, by some angry and over zealous Jews. Whilst being repeatedly stoned,Steven looked to the heavens and proclaimed Jesus Christ.

Secondly,the apostle Peter. The apostle Peter, was regarded as something of a hot head. Peter wasted no time, swinging his deadly sword and taking off the ear of Malchus ;which was later healed by Jesus Christ.

When it came to his crucifixion, the apostle Peter, deemed himself unworthy; to be crucified like his beloved Lord. Peter, wanted to be crucified upside down, as a mark of respect to his master. The love and devotion, shown by these early saints, is truly remarkable. My only request is this. Almighty God, bless me with a portion of courage; as these sincere saints of old, Amen.

SOCIETY V US

We are living at a time, where shootings and stabbings are extremely common. There was a time, when the only thing a doorman had to worry about; was a cosh or a knife. Now, with the emergence of gangs roaming the streets, there's an altogether different problem; the gun.

Along with the regular threats of, "ill be back", there is now the "I'm gunner shoot ya" brigade. This by itself, is certainly nothing new, as revenge and reprisals go hand in hand. What makes things different nowadays however, is guns are easily acquired.

The threats being dished out nowadays, can quite easily be carried out. There was a time,when only the genuine gangsters had guns. Nowadays folks, anyone can get one. When I take a bus ride and decide to sit upstairs, I feel sad at the conversations I hear. The youth are engrossed in topics, which, glamourise killing and violence. Practically all of them seem to discuss shootings and stabbings and who's going to get who.

What worries me most, is the way in which, they actually seem to glorify violence. I was privy to a conversation, which took place on a public bus. The conversation was between a black youth called Bazz and a white youth called Steve. When I left the bus, all I could do was shake my head. The conversation, went as follows.

"So what you been up to Bazz?

Nothing much Steve, just dossing, tried looking for some graft, but nothings out there.

Kevs just come out the nick Steve, what a crazy xxxx he is.

You're a bit of a nutter aren't you Steve, remember when you took that kids nose off in school,

Yeah Bazz proper battered him, blood every where, teachers had to call the old man to get me.

Have you calmed down now Steve?

You mad ! I got kicked out the Zanzibar club Saturday night and ended up in a boozer on Broad St.

What happened in Broad St Steve?

Some bloke upset me, so I bottled him; I stuck the broken bottle in his face, blood every where.

A bloke in is thirties tried to rugby tackle me, my mate said he was CID, we proper leather-ed him.

We ran down Broad Street laughing, I was covered head to toe in blood, I proper flipped it. I would of have had it with anyone that night, trust me.

What you up to later Steve,

You know the retail park near Sheldon Bazz, its getting proper robbed tonight".

I watched as Steve built a spliff and listened as they reminisced about the smoking sessions, they enjoyed at school. The conversation was dominated, with talk of drugs, prison, robbing, stabbing and basically all things negative; my bus stop approached, so I left.

I mentioned before. As a youth, I always imagined being in films like the warriors or bad boys. I can honestly say however, I never sought the part of a cold blooded killer. Being the ruthless psychopath,who gave no mercy, certainly never appealed to me. I was the adrenalin junky, who enjoyed the battle, the excitement and the victory.

What we have today, is a generation of youth; who think being bad, is good. With the influence of certain artists in the music industry, the youth seem hypnotised. The almost continuity, of very violent songs, fills a persons mind, with unbalanced aggression. Is it really any wander, some of our youth today,walk the violent path. Not only do some walk that path,but they do it, with such arrogance.

In the seventies and eighties, music was generally a medium; which promoted fun, love and happiness etc.

Could you ever imagine, Duran Duran, having a shoot out with Abba. Or Paul Weller, singing about shooting kajagoogoo. The thought is so ridiculous, you should be locked up for having it. This example,may seem a bit way out there, but ask your self the question; am I making a point ?

Have any Hip Hop artists, ever been involved, in extreme violence and shootings ? Not only that,is it uncommon, for them to be at war, amongst themselves?

What do we hear certain Hip Hop artists rapping about. Not all of them of course,but a lot, 'shoot the xxxx, no one xxxx with me', and so it goes on. Is it any wander, with the audience they attract, that a lot of youth today are hostile. Society, now as to try its best, to deal with this disrespectful generation. Or in a door-persons case, turn them away from the establishment.

I was watching the television recently and saw a sight, that sent shivers down my spine. it was the image of a person, who had unfortunately lost their sight.

The news report, was about a young 23 year old male, named Carl. The report stated, Carl had gone out for the evening, with some friends. They had all gone to a local pub in Derby, the Crown and Cushion.

The evening was drawing to a close, so the group had decided to leave and call it a night. I remember in his interview, Carl saying, "some of my friends were standing across the road, in dispute, so I went across, to make sure they were OK"

Before he knew what was happening, Carl was struck with a blow of such ferocity ; everything around him went black. Carl's world was to be turned upside down. He recalls at the time, lying on the floor, with someone cradling his head and comforting him.

The blow to Carl's face, was struck with such force, that is his right eye; is now permanently damaged. What makes this story really upsetting though is; Carl had suffered an accident as a boy, which had left him totally blind in his left eye. From learning to live as a partially sighted man; he must now overcome life, as a totally blind young man. If coming to terms with one accident wasn't bad enough, he now as to cope with two. Carl as had to leave Derby, leave his friends and give up the job he had recently enjoyed. He now lives with his mother,in another part of the country; and his life will never be the same again.

Carl's case is a very sad one, due to the fact he was partially blind already, was probably the main reason, this case became televised news. This type of assault however, is extremely common. In this unstable society in which we live in and with the type of people it produces, by know means is it surprising.

An elderly friend once told me, if you keep chasing fairness in life, you end up running, for a very long time. A statement which is quite sad, but unfortunately very true.

I was the original eighties man. It was during this period, that I started to learn about life. I learned about the bad things and all the good things it brought. The music of the era, that did it for me, was acid rave, dance music and house.

I can remember with fondness, getting ready to go out with the lads and the pride we would all take in our appearance. At the time, we all had double breasted, navy blazers. They were accompanied with, beige trousers and moccasins. We would all meet in the Rock Pub, which was in Saltley. We would have a few beers, then head into town.

The smart dress and pride of the eighties, is lost amongst the lads of today. Style, as sadly been replaced, by extortionately priced, designer clothes. Which more often than not, are made in a run down factory, in Thailand.

Back in the eighties, I wouldn't dream of wearing jeans on a night out. The truth is, you would be too embarrassed to even think it. When we first started going out, there was normally Kevin aka Caines, Wayne aka Bass, Patrick, Batson and I. As time went by, our group of a few, grew to about twenty; with the rest of Saltley joining the group.

The sudden influx, wasn't due to our popularity, it was more a case of the fights we had. At the end of the day, all the lads wanted to join our merry band.

I was the youngest of the group, but quickly learned, everything I needed to know. I must say, before I go any further, we certainly weren't angels. We would play up with the best of them and if a fight was in the offing, we wouldn't refuse it.

What I am proud of however is, we never bullied people, or picked on the defenceless. If we had any trouble, it was often with like minded young men. Men who thought, a punch up, would be a nice way to finish the night. We were always smart and spent a lot of money replacing torn shirts. We never ever, carried knives on a night out. The thought of going clubbing, with a weapon in tow, was never entertained. We were happy go lucky young men, not angels by very a long way, but respectful.

As young men, what we whole hardheartedly possessed, was respect. We would never provoke, or interfere with a group; who wanted nothing more, than a pleasant night out.

The bullies and trouble makers of this generation, don't think twice about beating up an innocent bystander. Or even for that matter, stick a knife in someones belly. What makes matters worse, is collectively, they all possess the same mentality. They all feed off each others lust for blood and desire to impress.

I wouldn't for one second, try and paint a false picture of the eighties. It wasn't all about peace, love and harmony. What I will say however is this, things just aren't the same today.

The eighties was a time, when altercations and violence were plentiful. Football hooliganism was in its prime; but take it from me, when you went out for a drink, you'd never imagine being shot.

Doormen in the clubs and pubs of Birmingham, often had their work cut out. With the emergence of the sharp dressed man, who didn't mind getting his shoes dirty; the doormen always had to be on the ball. For whatever reason, back in the day; door staff always appeared firmer and certainly seemed bigger; especially if you were standing in punching distance.

I still see a few of the old school doormen, plying their trade. I always exchange a wry smile and a hand shake. Normally ending with, "your to old for this game son". It seems really weird, when I think back and can still recall their younger faces; some fifteen years ago. I can remember, when these guys would be standing on the door of Power House, or Pagoda Park; and on seeing my pals come round the corner, shrug their shoulders. They would often look to the heavens and sigh. They would have down cast expressions of 'oh no,I wanted an easy night'.

How ironic, that I now find myself doing the same job and thinking the same things they did. The only difference being, in my day, the doormen knew what to expect from us; and exactly what they were up against. We had pride and we fought very fair, by modern standards. Make no mistake, the doormen of that era, were no mugs and if need be; they certainly gave as good as they got.

I was talking to an old school doorman, called Neil; who I have mentioned before. Neil would often say, men were men in the early days. A fight would often be, fists, feet and head butts. You would sometimes get, the occasional knife being pulled,but very rarely. But nowadays, heaven only knows what's coming out.

I can clearly remember, going out with my pals during the eighties and getting into trouble. The only weapon, you had access to, was a bottle, or a glass. The thought of a gun, or anything as sinister ;stayed in the movies, where they belonged.

I remember being in a pub, called Boogies wine bar; and a policeman got glassed. His eye was quite badly damaged, so it appeared in the evening mail. At the time, it was a fairly major event. A policeman, being seriously assaulted in a bar, was almost unheard of. The West Midlands Police wanted answers,and they wanted them now.

Whoever was responsible, would be without doubt, severely punished. It didn't take very long, before it was quickly associated with, the notorious football hooligans, the Zulu Warriors, of Birmingham City.

I smile to myself, because If the same thing happened today, you would be lucky to read it in the small print of the local circular. The truth is, it would now rate as trivial news and get very little exposure.

A very common site on the streets of Birmingham, are the youths in baggy jeans and baseball caps. In Birmingham, there are two rival gangs, the Burger Bar Crew and the Johnson Crew.

Whenever there is gun activity, around Handsworth, Aston, Perry Barr, and Newtown; they are suspects number one. Whether they are responsible or not, due to their reputations;they are always prime suspects. To be honest though, the way in which many of them behave, its not surprising.

A lot of these gangs, go to social venues, with a " I don't give a dam" attitude. They go to a door, with a no caps allowed policy and stand there wearing caps. You politely ask them to remove their caps, and you're looked at, as though their caps are stuck to their heads.

Doormen are scowled at, in the hope of inflicting fear. Staff are expected to tremble, and shake in sheer terror. When faced with these lads, you have to stand firm and in some cases, bite your lip. Their glares aren't frightening, the individuals aren't frightening; but the guns they carry, are very frightening.

This unfortunately,is where they have the upper hand; you can't go to work, wearing a firearm. Certain items you can get away with (metal torch) but a gun, that's asking a lot. Well,what can be done, you might ask. Without sounding to obvious, the simple answer is this, turn them away. If you're dealing with guys,whose sole aim is to cause trouble; keep the trouble, outside.

The next time you see them, turn them away again. If this means, you have to recruit more door staff, that's a small price to pay. No matter how many assurances you get, don't let them in.

Keeping them out, is far easier than getting them out, trust me. If they come to the door like lions, then once inside, they won't become pussy cats. At this point, the old saying comes into affect, you can take the man from the ghetto, but you can't take the ghetto from the man. Unless the man before you,as gone through a born again experience of sorts ;don't expect bad,to suddenly turn good.

I remember a typical Thursday night at the pit stop. I chatted with the punters and then went for a patrol through the bar. I noticed four unsavoury characters, who had trouble, stamped all over them. They sported padded coats, hooded tops, and black gloves. They were bad boys personified, or so they thought.

The night drew on, and one lad in particular; kept deliberately putting his cap on and then taking it off. The rules of the bar were clear, no caps, or drugs allowed. I approached the lad and told him to remove his cap and stick to the rules. He gave me a stupid excuse of his hair looks messy and well out of shape.

I smiled to myself and thought, that's a problem for you and your barber ;either way, you're not wearing your cap. There were always three of us working the bar and in truth, it wasn't enough. The bar was very popular and always attracted a large crowd. More often than not, we were always needed at the front door; to monitor the continuous traffic of the punters.

This was a situation, I was never too pleased with; as my job, was to stay inside and keep an eye on the crowds. looking out for potential problems,was what I did best;and stopping any potential trouble, before it flared up.

The evening was going well and the door was under control, so I took a little wander around the bar. I could smell some drugs in the air, but wasn't sure where it was coming from. I noticed the cap man again, with cap glued to his head; so I told him to remove it, he smiled and waltzed off. I wandered to myself, does this kid think he's in the play ground. What on earth is going on in his head, I thought. Are we now playing, the catch me with my cap on game; I wasn't impressed.

To be honest, this guy was really getting on my nerves. My boss had mentioned his cap to him; on several occasions. The lad was blatantly doing as he pleased and quite frankly, trying it on.

Pete the boss mentioned, the bar staff smelt some drugs. The aroma was drifting from one of the concealed corners of the bar. Pete was pretty sure, it was cap man and his lads. He asked me to take a look. Pete was a smart cookie, who had worked in all sorts of pubs around the country. From is experiences in Manchester, he knew the sort of group, we were dealing with. As I left him, he said "if you see the usual suspects, don't jump in".

It was ten forty-five pm and we finished at eleven. Pete said, "If it is them, just let them know your there". I knew straight away, cap man and his followers; would be at the heart of any problems. I strolled through the Pit Stop and it came as no surprise; tucked away in a corner of the bar, was the cap man himself. He was stinking the place out with drugs. Seeing the behaviour of these guys, and acting like the world owed them something, troubled me.

I wanted nothing more, than to get assistance and throw them out on their ear. Pete said "we shut in fifteen minutes, so on this occasion, let it go". Pete went on, "When they leave tonight, they wont be coming in again; so let them have their little moment".

Part of me was far from happy, dealing with trouble was what he paid me for; but I knew exactly where he was coming from. On leaving the bar, cap man and his friends, nodded at me. I was no fan of theirs, as much as they were no fan of mine. One thing I never do, is encourage these forced up bad boys; into thinking I'm happy with them. I watched them go and knew they would be back; it would only be a matter of time.

No two ways about it I thought; when they returned, a point would definitely be made. With the end result,being made crystal clear to all of them. It would plainly be, guys, you're not welcome, not wanted, or at all impressive.

I knew I would see them again, but there would be no way on earth ; they would be allowed back into the bar. There was no way whatsoever, they'd get the opportunity, to treat the place like they owned it. They may have got away with it once, but believe you me; it wouldn't happen again.

These boys needed to realise, we ran a decent bar in Brindley place; not a run down bar, in the Bronx. A week passed by and as predicted, they came back. Pete was in Florida, but before he left, we discussed these guys. It was made crystal clear, by any means necessary, I was to keep them out. They had marched towards the door, with a disgusting attitude; and needed to be taught, a harsh lesson in life.

As was expected, the following week they appeared; and the conversation, was no surprise.

"You're not coming in guys" I said it in an assertive tone. This was met with "why, why, what we done blood, what we done"? I refreshed their memories,concerning last weeks performance, and told them they had their fun ; and for them, the party was over.

They stood there looking at each other, getting smaller and smaller by the minute. The tension was now rising and I could sense they weren't quite sure how to proceed. The punters in the queue, were watching intently, waiting for someone to quake. They knew these lads were trouble and wouldn't appreciate, being put under the bad boy spotlight. As predicted, the bravado started, let us in, we did nothing wrong, you got the wrong guys, and so on.

I had been here before and the last thing I was going to do,was get drawn into an endless conversation. I made myself crystal clear. "Last week, you had your fun, you put caps on your head; like silly little kids". I continued "You smoked drugs in front of the boss and to be perfectly honest, you're not wanted in here". I went onto finish our conversation with "take it from me boys, you're not getting in".

They tried in vain, to plead a case which wasn't there and when the penny finally dropped; they took out their mobile phones, calling for help. These so called bad boys, needed reinforcements.

They trotted off, with caps on heads, and angry expressions. Vexed threats were shouted towards us, "we'll be back".The night carried on as normal, but when you deal with a certain type of crew, you never truly relax. The thought of a cowardly attack, is always lingering about.

Fighting is one thing, when it starts, you know how to deal with it; but waiting around for a potential fight, is totally different.

When a fight kicks off, you often go into automatic pilot and react in a way, which as become natural to you. When you have to think about a potential fight, the mind starts throwing up all kinds of different scenarios. You have often fought the fight, with twenty, when in reality, only four may return.

If I see a group of lads, approaching the door and they walk with a bouncy step, have hoods over faces and have a solitary glove on hand; my first impression is trouble. That trouble, my fellow door team, is with a capital T. It may sound judgmental, but I couldn't care less. If people dress like bad boys, act like bad boys, talk like bad boys and make threats like bad boys; then in my humble opinion, there not, good Samaritans.

As far as I'm concerned, if I let them through the door of my pub, I deserve all the problems, that come with it. I would consider myself a fool, who is quite frankly, encouraging trouble; and a hard night's work.

We are doormen, not fortune tellers. We can't see the hidden contents, of an overcoat. Unless, you get the opportunity to frisk someone, you can never be sure what their carrying. The cliche reads, you can't judge a book by its cover; but in some cases, believe you me, you can. Some people, stink of trouble. If they feel the need, to hide their faces with a hood, then the educated guess is, they may well be.

GOADING

Goading a doorman, can be done mentally, as well as verbally. I will try and explain this more deeply.

It was a bank holiday Sunday. I was working a three till six shift, by myself, and then being joined by another doorman, at seven. The afternoon had gone smoothly, and after taking advantage of the pub menu, I prepared my self for the evening to come.

Bank holiday week ends, are traditionally busy and are often prone to trouble. This is largely because, not many people work the Monday, so they make it a priority, to get drunk. Many go out their way, to simply get, well and truly smashed.

During this particular period of drunkenness, the attitude adopted by many is, stay out of my way (or else) This was the type of punter I expected, the only difference being, Aston Villa Football Club, were also playing that day. I didn't envy spending all afternoon and night; dealing with alcohol charged, football fans.

Due to the busy week end, we charged £5 pound entrance fee. On top of this, we charged £1 a drink, so consequently, we were full to the rafters.

At ten pm, two lads came to the door, wanting entry. I told them we were full and this was met with an ice cold glare. I waited for the inevitable insults, but surprisingly they walked away. I know you shouldn't judge a book by the cover, but one lad, was tall and scruffy; while the other, was a big fat skinhead. This particular chap, wore an England shirt, which barely covered is belly. My senses told me, these lads were trouble, and I was glad to see them go.

We exercise a policy of, no sports caps, or football shirts in the bar; so even if we wasn't packed, they would have been refused entry. Ten thirty pm now approached; and the bar was packed, both inside and out. Every where you turned, punters were either throwing up, or stumbling around drunk. How no one fell in the canal, still remains a mystery to this day.

Bearing all this in mind, the evening was going relatively smoothly. Considering the amount of punters drinking, and the fact there were only two of us working; things were running relatively well. Deep down though, I knew this was too good to be true and it would only be a matter of time; before something would surface.

My negative mind, must have cast a spell, because as if by magic, the two chaps who were refused entry, emerged from the crowd. They had pints in hand and grins on faces. I couldn't believe it, there standing with a group of lads, were these two thug looking characters.

They somehow came back undetected and mingled in with the crowd. One of their friends, obviously got them their beer.

Kevin, the doorman I was working with, said he'd deal with it, and had a brief word. Ten minutes later, they were still there, drinking and laughing away; with the rest of their mob. They stood rooted to the spot and showing no signs of budging; this time, we both approached them.

I hoped for good, as you always do, but, was prepared for bad, as you always should be. The ten metre walk was made, "finish your drinks, then you have to go lads". This was met with 'yeah yeah yeah'. Tall man looked at me, none too impressed; with a try and make me expression. The lads they were with, were hangers on, the sort who get miraculously brave in numbers.

My eyes were fixed on tall man. I had already weighed him up, he was six foot one, with a rather large chin. I repeated what Kevin had said, but added an assertive "OK" at the end of it. We went back to the door and waited.

This is where, the mental goading comes into effect. We've told these lads to drink up and leave and there they are, sipping away, at zero m-p-h. There making a point, of taking forever to finish their beer.

Kevin said "I thinking we'll be fighting with these", I nodded my head and agreed. I stood there thinking OK; you'll get what you come for. The pre- fight nerves had already started, the focus was well and truly together, all that was left now, was the next move.

The slow drinking, is the equivalent of, you've told me to drink up, but watch me, I'm not rushing. I'm taking as long as I want, so what you going to do, the balls in your court. Kevin had been on his mobile, and a couple of his friends appeared. If the two guys and there hangers on, thought they were dealing with two, they would soon realise, they weren't.

I said to Kevin "its time to sort it" Kevin said "wait". We stared towards them, their time was rapidly running out. The goading pair, as I will call them, were starting to look nervous; they could see what was coming. A couple of their entourage, were now looking towards us, very sheepishly to say the least.

The beers that had taken so long to supp, suddenly seemed to vanish with ease. They gulped their drinks, like men on a dessert island and walked away, without a second look. The situation came to an end, without the physical being used. Excellent I thought, thank God.

I know some readers, would have been reading this scenario and expecting a right tear up as the outcome. I can honestly say, fortunately it didn't come to this. The fighter inside the fighter, isn't always as tough,as the fighter looks.

Point A, you see the problem, point B you deal with it. Between point A and point B, you make a decision, fight or flight, face the foe, or turn away. The state of mind you adopt, will make all the difference. If the situation is sorted peacefully and without any incident, then excellent. The desired outcome as been achieved, praise God.

There are times when you give people the benefit of the doubt, then quickly realise, how wrong you've been. It was another Bank holiday Sunday, it was seven o'clock, so we opened the door and started letting people in. I was talking to Neil and another doorman and generally taking things as they come. We saw two lads coming our way and thought nothing of it, they looked like they'd had a few, but we allowed them in. Within five minutes of ordering their drinks, they were dancing away and splashing beer. I said to Neil, I best stop this before it starts, watch my back. I went over to the one closest to the bar and said "after that lads, you've got to go" I explained, they can finish their drinks, get their admission fee back; but they have to go.

The debating started, with a drunken hand being pushed out. "Come on man,don't be out of order," they said. It was a very big mistake, to have even let them in. I didn't want to get physical, unless there was no choice left. "You can finish the beers lads, but this isn't the place for you".I said.

The one lad who was closest to me, started looking at me, with a look of ; we go when were ready, so have some of that. I thought to myself, here we go again. You try and show a little bit of leeway and it's thrown right in your face. Basically, they didn't give a hoot. I gave Neil the nod and with the assistance of another doorman, we ejected them. The doors opened at seven, they were out by ten past. We had stopped a potential problem, before it had started; and were certainly more vigilant, for the rest of the night.

When you work the door, its normal for your mates to visit the pub. They would usually have a little chat and a couple of beers. On one occasion, it was a friend of a friend, who caused the problems.

I was working with Reuben and his mate Barry came to the pub. This was normal, I had met Barry on a number of occasions and he was a good chap. Barry had brought a pal with him, who he introduced to Reuben and so the night went on. The evening went well,so all the punters left merry and very fulfilled.

My shift was over, so I pulled up a chair and started to relax. I watched the barges, sail along the canal; while sipping a double Jack Daniels & coke.

I saw Reuben outside talking to Barry and his mate, and thought nothing of it. Ten minutes later, Reuben came into the bar and pulled up a seat. I could see something was troubling him, so I asked him what was up. "I was going knock that guy out", Reuben said,he was referring to Barry's mate. "What's he done"? I asked. Reuben went on to tell me, the bar staff had seen him, trying to sell drugs and had told Pete.

The boss Pete, was a good friend of mine and not one to turn a blind eye; on dealings involving drugs. Especially dealings, that jeoperdised his licence. He took his licence very seriously and understandably, didn't want the name of his bar tarnished.

No wander Reuben was annoyed. This guy was let in, on the back of his friendship with Barry. The guy had taken a blatant liberty; and on top of all this, he was trying to sell drugs in the pub.

What disrespect I thought to myself. The bar was very well run and one thing we never tolerated, was drug selling. Barry told Reuben, he had no idea what the guy was doing and can only apologise for his behaviour. Reuben spoke to the guy, and told him in no uncertain terms, "never show your face in here again".I told Reuben, I understand how he feels, but at the end of the day; he wasn't to blame. On this occasion, you have to let it go.

This was one of those unfortunate situations, which sometimes occurs. The only person to blame, is Barry's mate and at the end of the day, he's no child. He knew exactly what he was doing, so an apology in all honesty, seems very shallow.

You can't mind read people, so an incident like this, is just one of those things. One things for sure though, he never came back to the Pit Stop, ever again.

MAKE A DIFFERENCE

More often than not, people got to work, do their job and become very much robotic; in their behaviour. I don't say this in a judgmental way, as I was very much the same. If we realised, as security staff on the front line, the difference a conversation could make; we would look at work in a very different light.

When I was a rowdy teenager, going to town and causing trouble, I would often be lectured to, by certain doormen. The funny thing is, the doormen I respected in the 1980s-90s, I still respect now, When I look back at their past advice and rebukes, so many yeas ago, I have to smile. At the time, they may have felt they were wasting their breath, or beating their head against a wall; but believe you me, they weren't.

I took on board a lot of the comments that were made and without realising it; they were planting a seed of responsibility and wisdom. The very fact, I can still remember conversations from many years ago, shows their value.

A lot of the old school doormen, were simply employed as muscle enforcers. They weren't hired, because of their flowing articulate conversations, they were there to stop trouble. Due to this sort of expectation and position, many doormen, kept them selves to themselves; and only engaged with punters, on a not so friendly basis.

The stern and steadfast appearance of some, was naturally off putting. A stereo type, in the minds of many, was almost instantly formed. A large number of bouncers, were given no encouragement to change. I find this a real shame, as some of the old school doormen I know, are well educated and bright in conversation. Some have a wealth of knowledge and have very good advice to share.

I wouldn't expect doormen, to suddenly become agony aunts, because first and foremost, their job is one of security etc. I do believe however, certain positive actions, can improve a battered image; or enhance,a flagging reputation.

I read an article in a national newspaper,which sheds a little light, into what I mean; it was titled, Callous Beyond Belief and read as follows;

Cruel Christina Ribas, left her baby girl in a freezing car, for more than five hours, while she went clubbing in a local night spot.

Ribas aged 28, strapped the 18 month old tot, who was wearing shorts and a flimsy top, into her VW Golf and parked it outside the club.

As temperatures fell to -2C the student boozed and danced the night away, before staggering out of the club at 2.20 am to drive home.

A concerned bouncer, who tried to stop drunken Ribas from entering the car, was horrified when he saw the little baby in the back seat. Police were called and Ribas was arrested outside the Elemental club in Manchester.

Last night Ribas was behind bars, after she was jailed for 3 months for child cruelty and failing to provide a breath test.

Judge Alan Berg said "this is one of the most shameful episodes of child cruelty by neglect; I have had the misfortune to deal with, in my ten years on this bench. It was an act of pure selfishness, nothing more, nothing less. The facts of this case beggars belief. If it was an animal left locked in the car in these conditions, there would be a justifiable public outrage, how much more for a little baby?"

The judge added; "it was a particularly cold night, the baby was in the back of the car, scantily dressed, in the middle of the city centre, in the early hours of the morning. You in my view, abandoned all your natural instincts and responsibilities. The only reason you did, was to indulge in your desire to have a good time."

Club assistant manager Mervyn Lewis said, his staff had been stunned to see the baby in the back of the car. He said "I recognised the woman as one of our regulars and noticed she was staggering about a bit. I told the Bouncers to stop her getting into her car and called the police. The Bouncers took the keys off her, but she became aggressive and started attacking them. None of us knew at this stage that there was a baby in the car. I had gone back to the bar when I was told, so I went down to look, it was the kind of thing you had to see for yourself to believe."

Manchester magistrates' court, had heard how Portuguese born Ribas, who admitted the charges, had left the baby without food or drink. Passers by did not notice the tot, because of the cars blacked out windows. Defence solicitor Jeremy Spence said, Ribas from Salford, had never been in trouble before and had not intended to stay in the club for such a long time.

When I first read this article, the conduct of the mother, upset me. In situations like this, I always examine the worse case scenario. In this case, it would be the mother entering the car, driving off and encountering a fatal collision.

The bouncers involved in this event, should be congratulated for stopping a potentially sad situation. The news paper heading, could have been far graver; than simply "callous mother". For the sake of an alcoholic buzz and a good time, two lives could have been lost for nothing. One would have been brought about through ill discipline, the other; because life gave them a selfish mother.

There are many situations, where you don't have to go beyond your call of duty; but life sometimes, gives you little choice.

During the early nineties, I worked at a night club called Bonds, with a friend called Gary Twist. The club as now changed its name, to

H20. The two years I spent there, were very enjoyable, as door work goes. There was very little violence, or serious aggro to note.

Miss Money Pennies, the well known dance syndicate; had a Saturday night slot, so the place was regularly filled with dancers. I remember sitting on my stool in my regular position, and noticed what appeared to be an altercation at the bar. As I approached, I saw a girl shaking vigorously and quickly realised, something was seriously wrong. I managed to support her back, just before she fell, and lowered her gently to the ground. It was clearly obvious by now, that she was having some form of fit. I had no medical experience in this filed, so I just knelt over her, making sure her head didn't bang against the floor.

This seemed to go on for an eternity, but thankfully it stopped.

The young lady sat upright and I lifted her to her feet. I lead her to a quiet spot and asked if there was anything I could do. She said she was a diabetic and had forgotten her injection, so consequently was running low on the necessary medicines. I was joined by another doorman called Carter, who suffered form the same thing. He reassured her as best he could and told her he knew exactly how she felt. She was given something to give her a boost and when all was done, she felt more embarrassed; about being lowered to the ground.

The crowd which had gathered, were told to disappear and leave her in peace. For the rest of the night, she got the red carpet treatment. The young lady, was reassured in a funny sort of way; that her back was covered. Thankfully for all involved, there were no more issues and the problem free night, remained problem free.

It would have been easy to have disappeared, after helping her up; and leaving her to her own devices. At the end of the day, we have a personal responsibility, not only as doormen, but as human beings. Some doormen, through fear of doing something wrong, or personal embarrassment; would have chosen the disappearing path.

I would go as far to say, that more than 50% of doormen; don't have first aid at work certificates. This could be an exaggerated percentage, but I look at myself, as an example. Throughout my time as a doormen, I was never first aid qualified.

With all the changing laws and European objectives, it is only a matter of time, before along with being licensed; doormen will be be first aid trained. In the trendy city centre bars of town, a lot of landlords, place priority on appearance. They often judgmentally associate, the flat nosed doormen, as something from the past. I sincerely believe, the responsibility of being a doorman, will drastically change; and a serious re -vamping will take place.

One of the funniest situations I have encountered, was when I had to pull a punter, out of a canal. The Pit Stop bar, as I stated before, runs along side a canal. For many unfortunate revelers, who can't hold their beer, it's a very unwelcome site.

Bank holiday Sunday was upon us again, the bar was packed and the £1 bottles of beer, were going down well. Tied outside the bar, were three, very pristine barges. I stood looking at the barges, and out from the barges, emerged four not so pristine men.

It was now seven o'clock and the chances of getting into any drinking establishments, were zero.

On a scale of one to ten, they were dressed about five. Due to the fact, I had seen them before, I overlooked their appearance; and allowed them entry. As the night went on, the cheap drinks started to take their toll; and at about ten thirty, Pete made an appearance. He drew my attention, to one of the men I had let in and asked me to get rid.

The bloke was some what drunk and though harmless, was becoming something of a nuisance. I approached him at the bar and told him the situation; he smiled, shook my hand and headed for the front door. He had been given a good run for his money, so wasn't complaining. The chap said goodbye and nodded his head.

I watched as he walked towards his barge, his balance was far from foot perfect. I thought to myself, hes only got ten metres to walk, he'll be fine. A little sad, at seeing him leave, I turned and walked back to the bar. I took two or three steps, then froze; I heard a noise that I didn't want to hear and quickly turned round.

The laughing and jesting, that had previously filled the air; stopped with a splash! My worse scenario was coming to pass, the chap had fallen into the canal "oh no" I shouted.

He had climbed onto the roof of his barge and due to the effects of the beer swilling around in his head, had lost his balance. He went onto do, a very bad impression, of a Bay Watch lifeguard and fell in the canal. I saw one punter lying on the top of the barge, with his hand extended. I wasted no time and dived on the top of the barge and followed suit. The chap next to me, grabbed his left hand and I grabbed the right.

I remember, the drenched pony tailed figure, staring up at me; and grinning like a Cheshire cat. Believe you me, this was no laughing matter. The effort it took to haul him up, was immense.

He was about thirteen stone and coupled with his drenched crombi coat, he weighed a ton.

When we eventually got him out, he stood up, gave a little speech and began laughing. The fact he had nearly drowned and given me a heart attack, was oblivious to him.

Reuben and Kurt the other doormen, were laughing their sox off. Reuben had contemplated diving in, but after seeing the dark and dingy water, thought against it.

I can honestly say, my first thoughts were, good night Vienna. Seeing him surface and grinning his head off, was a very welcome site and one I certainly wont forget. Praise God.

ONE MAN DOOR, A ROTTEN SCORE

I have never been a fan, of the one man door. Whenever I go for an evening out: and the pub as a solitary doorman at the front, I always feel a bit sorry for them. I cant help being concerned, for the individuals well being.

Should punters start behaving badly; what chance is there for the lone doorman. Should a fight break out, or a group of punters, start turning over tables ;its near impossible to quell the eruption.

In a job, where you often need assistance, and colleagues to watch your back; you shouldn't be working single handed.

If a situation occurs which leaves you no option, but to deal with it by yourself, then that's unfortunate, and one of those things.

However, when you're not given any choice, and end up being sent to a rough pub to work; then in my eyes, that's very, very dangerous.

In the middle of Birmingham city centre, there is a pub called the yard of ale. This is an old fashion pub, where you have to walk downstairs, to gain access to the bar. Once in the bar, due to the dungeon type location, there is no mobile reception, so cell phones become useless.

On match days, lads would meet up and have a drink before kick off; so the pub would often get packed. On the odd occasion, rival supporters would stop by, so you can imagine the atmosphere.

This pub, normally employs one doorman, who sits at the top of the stairs. This individual, as to deal with the punters, as they enter the premises. Once inside, the punters are basically left to their own devices, and are expected to behave maturely.

I don't say that in a bad way, as the doorman can't be in two places at the same time; so stopping trouble coming in, becomes his main priority.

I often wander, if the doorman as ever asked his boss, why hes the only man working there. When you've worked the door for a certain amount of time, you start to appreciate the importance, of having your back covered. In a one man bar, unless your one of the locals, your backs your own.

When a boss, sends one of his lads to a site, It pays to look at the pubs history and have an idea, about the clientele. When you're expected to deal with violence single handed, because someone as decided, their not wiling to pay for extra security; then you need to ask yourself the question why, and who benefits.

A lot of bosses nowadays, run their door companies, and have suspect lads working for them. Some, but fortunately not all, couldn't care less about them. If there's an opportunity, to make some money from an individuals presence, believe you me, they'll do it. Regardless of the consequences.

Broad St, is the pub and club capital of Birmingham. If you're observant, you'll notice practically every bar, is run by a different door company. In terms of personal finance, it's a good thing; it gives you the opportunity, to earn a fair living. It also increases, your opportunities; of regular employment.

The down side however is, men being employed and working for the minimum wage. The boss of the company, has undercut the competition ;and if you pay peanuts, you'll get monkeys.

Fortunately for me, I'm in a position where I mostly work private, and have no main boss to answer to. At this stage of my life, I don't have to take what I'm given. If I don't like a pub, I simply don't work it.

I'm often told, I'm too much of a thinker, and always look at the worse case scenarios. I must admit, at times this can well be true. But at the end of the day, if I was an employer and had staff working for me, priority number one is, they're looked after. I would certainly make sure, my staff are not left in situations; where they could get annihilated.

Call me old fashioned, but I still believe in loyalty. Sending someone into a situation, which could prove fatal, is disloyal. Like I said before, I'm a bit of a thinker, but trust me; I know where my heart is. I can only assume, this situation is brought about by greedy companies. Who sadly put their profit margin, before the desire of quality staff.

KNIFE CRIME

Imagine, being confronted by a person,with a six inch blade. I remember, a good friend of mine, called Junior Reeves aka toffee. We would often shoot pool together and have a beer in the Rock Pub. A few months had passed and I hadn't seen Junior about; then I bumped into a friend, called Robert aka Cat.

I asked Robert about Junior and was given a sad answer, "Elvis, hes dead".Apparently Junior got into a knife fight and was fatally stabbed. Cat told me,when the ambulance came,Junior spoke to the paramedic and asked the question, "am I dieing"?

On hearing that,my only hope hope is; Junior sought forgiveness.

Juniors family, go to my brothers church, so he was very aware of forgiveness. I only hope, in Juniors moment of reflection, he cried out to God for mercy. If this is the case and I sincerely hope it is,the wonderful God I serve, always forgives.

THE DANGERS

Sometimes when I work the door, people come up to me and say, "I'd love to do your job, standing at the door and eying up the women".Some would also say, "you doormen,getting phone numbers all night,what an easy job you have".

These lads are sadly misguided; and have never experienced violence at its most frightening. I hazard a guess, they have never been in a situation, where they thanked God, they were still alive.

I liken these guys, to armchair boxers. They watch the big fights and spend their night,slating all the fighters. Regardless of the fact, the boxer is battered,bruised and extremely fatigued. To the armchair critic,this is simply immaterial. These are the viewers, who love to shout insults and abuse; and in their hearts, think they can do better.

The truth is however, they wouldn't last the training; let alone the round. So all you would be doormen out there,who think the job is a cake walk, think again.

I was talking to a friend of mine, big Steve Williams; who works the door in Burton on Trent. Steve told me of a very sad story; which took place, some time ago. The story goes as follows.

There was a doorman working a bar, in a fairly rough area, two lads came to his door and for whatever reason, were turned away.

He continued his night as normal, expecting no repercussions. When his shift had finally finished, he ordered a taxi and waited for its arrival.

The taxi pulled up and in the car he went. I can just imagine the chap, sitting in the taxi, shirt collar open and bow tie off. Body relaxing and plans for the forthcoming day in his mind. The list is endless.

I hazard a guess, he was probably looking forward to a good nights rest, or a quick whiskey, before bed time. Sadly for him however, this wasn't to be the case.

The two cowards, he had refused entry, had etched a wicked plan. They were now laying in wait and seeking revenge. They knew where he lived and made their way to his house. Once there, the desire to get even, took over. They waited for the unsuspecting doorman to arrive and attacked.

He got to his destination, sadly unprepared for what was to come; and before he could get out the taxi, the demons pounced. He was set upon in a frenzied attack, that showed no signs of abating. I can only imagine, the frightened look of shock on his face. I can only guess, at what must of gone through his mind; when the two knife wielding maniacs, stood before him.

So here he was, a big weight lifting doorman; caught between the open taxi door. The doorman was repeatedly and mercilessly stabbed. On top of this, he was punched continuously.

The taxi driver, had to pull him to safety and speed off in the opposite direction. He drove towards the nearest hospital, in the hope of emergency treatment.

My friend went on to say, the bloke had been with is girlfriend, a very long time. When they eventually got married, he walked down the aisle,with the assistance of crutches. Sadly, the crutches have become a part of his every day life and he will never be the same again. The injuries he sustained in the knife attack, have left him physically hindered forever; but thankfully, they never took is life. Thank God.

One of the regulars at the Pit Stop, is an ex doorman called Chris. The desire to the wear the black suit again, as become his number one priority. He always says "the minute I get my door licence, I'll be straight back in the game mate". I always say to him, "you must be mad Chris,after what you went through, most people would retire; without a second thought". Chris always laughs. For a man who was put in intensive care, he certainly isn't put off.

This is Chris' story. He was working the door, in a club in Mylton kenes. The night was drawing to a close, so everyone, was finishing off their drinks. The doormen were doing the regular things and getting themselves ready for the "drink up lads, see you next week" line. Chris says, he approached a lad and politely said "drink up mate". For whatever reason, the lad took offence to this and started misbehaving.

A simple request of 'drink up' seemed to be taken very personally. The lad eventually departed and left with the famous terminator line "I'll be back". Threats to door-staff, are common; but whenever I receive a threat, I take it very seriously. I'm often told to relax and not to over react "let it go Elvis, let it go" is often said.

Call it what you will. Personally, I like to feel safe at work and most definitely, after work. Its often after work, when the doormen finishes their shifts, that threats are often carried out.

Any way, Chris dismissed the threat, as a load nonsense; along with all the others, but how wrong he was.

A few weeks later, he was walking to his car; then without any warning, he was attacked. Just like the threat made, the lad was back; and his crow bar wasn't friendly. Chris suffered numerous injuries, damaged skull, cracked ribs and various scars.

The Doctors placed him in intensive care and for several weeks, it was touch and go. Fortunately, Chris pulled through and the cowardly attacker was brought to justice. In court, the judge asked Chris, if the person in question was present, the reply was "yes your honour, the evil man, is sitting right there", the finger of Chris, pointing in the direction of the man.

The case went on and the mallet came down, guilty was the overwhelming verdict. The punishment dealt out, was a sentence of five years jail.

Chris, unsurprisingly took some time out the door game; but the desire to work, as seemingly been rekindled. What people often say, must be true; and that is, doormen are a crazy breed.

I remember going out with my girl friend, to a club I once worked at, called Bonds.

The evening was going well, with the crowd rocking; to a live performance from Daniel Beddingfield. The club was ram packed, with numerous coach parties. They had all arrived, to enjoy a wonderful night of RnB. I was very surprised and thought, what a good night this is turning out to be. To be honest, I wasn't the greatest lover, of this type of modern soul music; Northern soul, was more my cup of tea.

Anyway, as two am approached, I noticed a group of lads, walking through the crowd. They had hoods on their heads and coats buttoned up. Why do these guys do it, I asked myself. It's sweltering and your shirts, sticking to your back. For goodness sake I thought, and in heat such as this. I looked at these guys, waltzing through the crowd; like men on an antarctic expedition and shook my head.

The constant soul, was definitely taking its toll, so we decide to leave. I said my goodbyes to my friends, followed by the doormen, and headed for the sack.

The next day, I had a phone call and couldn't believe my ears. One of the doormen, who was working at the club, had been shot in the leg. The same old sad story I'm afraid, young boys with guns, acting like men. They started trouble on the front door and when they found things weren't going their way, out came the automatics.

The doorman who got shot, was a friend of mine called Giles. Thankfully, he made a full recovery and is still here to tell the tale. Giles took it all in his stride, if you pardon the pun; and his leg, shows no ill effects.

I was working with Reuben, and got talking to his friend Barry. We started discussing the door game and the dangers that exist. Barry once worked at a pub called the Radleys, which is in Birmingham. He told me of a violent incident that took place, that led him to retire.

He was at the Radleys, working with another two doormen. There were a group of lads drinking, who had been there all day; so the alcohol was having the desired effect. He said to me, one of the lads was acting stupid, so he decided to have a quiet word.

This unfortunately never had the desired effect and things got physical, very physical. Before he knew what was happening, the lad and his gang, were all on top of him.

Fists and feet were flying towards him, all aimed, with the same bad intention. Every direction he chose to turn, was greeted with left and right combinations. Barry was caught in a human tornado and not a pretty sight.

Barry took a right old beating. Know matter how many times they struck Barry, he wouldn't buckle. "One thing I've got, is a good chin" he said. They couldn't knock me out, so they stabbed me instead.

Here you have a man, already outnumbered and getting a right old beating. If that wasn't bad enough; they still felt the need to pull their blades and use the Sheffield. For those who don't know, Sheffield is famous for its steel industry. When a person threatens to pull the Sheffield; what their actually saying is, get ready to taste their blade. Brief lesson over, let's get back to Barry.

I asked him, what happened to the other two doormen, didn't they try and help. Barry's answer was no. They disappeared, left me on my own; done a runner. In simple terms, left me for dead.

Barry escaped and as the opportunity to reflect. The beating and brush with the blade, prompted immediate retirement. Others sadly, have not been so lucky; and their second chance, as never come.

Whenever a hostile situation, is resolved without violence; consider it as a major victory. To be in such a dangerous job and retire unscathed, is more of an achievement; than we give ourselves credit for. Ask any doormen who has lost an eye, a nose, or been seriously hurt and I'm sure he will agree.

These few stories, are very harsh reminders, of the dangers faced by door staff. The door game as it highs, but sadly, life changing lows. Every time I have a trouble free night, I view it as a job well done and always give God thanks. Believe you me, I take nothing for granted.

GET ASSISTANCE

As a doorman, your objective, is to deal with situations; as quickly and as safely, as possible. When dealing with a problem, don't think to yourself, if I get assistance, it will be looked upon as weakness; that perception, is based on pride and can prove fatal. When faced with trouble, two heads are better than one. Never ever feel, you have to tackle a dangerous situation, by your self. Remember, you're a member of a team, use the players.

Another night at the Pit Stop, taught me the importance of always getting assistance; and not leaving any thing to chance. It was a typical Thursday night, busy as anything, beer flowing by the gallon. I was on the door and nothing spectacular was happening. A friend of Reuben, told me the toilet attendant, was getting some grief from a punter; and the atmosphere wasn't good. I mentioned to one of the bar staff, I was going to check the toilets, so the door will be manned by one doormen.

The first mistake I made, was not telling the doormen, where I was going. The second mistake was, approaching a potential trouble spot, single handed. When I got in the toilet, I saw two lads standing around the attendant, both were drunk; and staring into space.

On seeing me, the attendant pointed to a lad and said "that's the one who's been threatening me". Here I was, in a secluded toilet, with no radio. I was in a situation, where one or more of his pals, could easily get involved. I weighed things up and said "come with me mate, let's have a chat". Straight away, I was given the "what I have done, what have I done" ? I repeated, "Come with me and lets have a little chat".

Fortunately, the lad came out the toilet, without much problem; but this was to soon change.

As we got back into the bar area, he started tensing up. The lads attitude, started changing and he started to become very cocky. "Don't even go there, with that attitude",I said. "You've threatened to hit the attendant, its time to go". He looked at me, with eyes glazed and unsteady legs. I held him tightly and said to him "behave". He tried to put up resistance, but in his drunken state, it was pointless.

I started leading him to the exit door, when all of a sudden, a group of his friends appeared. "That's my mate, he's with us, what you doing to him" ? Fingers were being pointed at me and I felt a hand on my shoulder, causing me to look round. It was at this point, I realised to myself, I should never have gone to the toilet, without the aid of another doorman. It was too late for regrets, what was done, was done. I had got myself into this problem and I would get myself out.

By now, it was basically a case of, what happens, happens.

"He's going with me, if any one touches me again, they'll regret it" I got myself into survival mode and was basically letting them know. If they touched me again, expect fire works.

I dragged their mate away and ushered him through the exit door. Kevin saw me outside with this chap, so I gave him the run down of what had happened; and the lad was taken away. While we were outside, the lads friends came out, to see what was happening. This time, their attitude was totally different and they were very apologetic; on behalf of their friend. I singled out the lad, who had held my shoulder and basically told him, " thank your lucky stars, you let go".

The way I felt, I wanted retribution. I could feel myself getting angrier by the second. The thought of him grabbing my shoulder, was bugging me. Seeing him standing in front of me, made my anger rise. I took a deep breath,took charge of my emotions and told him to disappear.

Deep down, I was mad with myself, for allowing the situation to have occurred; and putting myself in unnecessary danger. Believe you me, it taught me a lesson, I would never, ever,forget.

I told Reuben, the encounter could of got very ugly, and turned out extremely violent. I knew deep down, the only person I could blame, was myself. I never let it happen again.

The person I had ejected, and is loud mouth mate, came back the following week. How on earth, they expected to be allowed entry, is beyond me. Kevin gave them their marching orders and they waltzed off, full of apologies.

The fact they came back to the Pit Stop, expecting entry, highlights the arrogance of today's youth. Not only that, but the blatant ways; in which people of today, demonstrate little respect.

Christmas, is always a time, for trouble. Grown men become kids and kids become babies. During the festive season, trouble is a stone cold certainty, and it's simply a case of, door-staff be ready.

The bar was packed to the rafters,with over three hundred plus punters. Everywhere you turned, people were trying to dance like John Travolta, on a bad day. With two doormen on the front and me on the in side, our work was certainly cut out.

I was standing by the door scanning the crowd, when my attention was drawn to a young lady. She was beckoning me towards her, with a very worried expression on her face. The closer I got to her, the more I realised, trouble was at hand. She pointed to her right and between the packed crowds, I saw what appeared to be, a mass brawl.

Experience taught me, not to charge in, so my first objective, was to open the exit doors; and shout for assistance. Reuben and a new doorman Steve, came running towards me; we headed straight to the trouble spot, and cut threw the crowd like butter.

Beer was all over the floor, making our footing dangerously unsteady. I felt a heavy tug on my coat, Reuben later told me, he had to grab me, because he nearly fell on his backside.

When we got to the brawl, lads fled in different directions. I noticed a stocky black guy and standing beside him, was a white guy. They looked more than guilty, so no time was wasted in throwing them out. Their misguided cheer leaders, stood shouting and protested their innocence. With two out the way, we went back in. Another two more, guilty participants, were dealt with.

There were still more lads to find, so with the aid of a couple of witnesses, we began sifting through the crowd. Another lad was found in the toilet and taken outside; he was one of the regulars and was never any trouble before.

We were working together as a team, all for one, and one for all, simple musketeer rules. Reuben was about five foot ten, Steve about five foot seven and me six foot one. We certainly weren't monsters, or the most intimidating of lads to look at. One thing I've learned however is this, when you work together, with the same approach and attitude; people take you seriously.

More doormen, from the bars close by, came and lent a hand. They obviously thought, we were having a major war. Fortunately, they weren't needed and satisfied that we had ejected the guilty parties, we got back to work.

The black guy, who was thrown out, was pleading his case; and with the support of some ladies, convinced us he was hard done by. We gave him the benefit of the doubt, and allowed him back in.

At this point, I decided to talk to the regular, who had been ejected; and hopefully, get some honest answers. He went on to say, a couple were arguing and he had glanced towards them. The lad who was arguing, shouted towards him; what are you looking at ? and went on to punch him. On being attacked, he did what most people would do, hit back.

Due to the slippery tiles, he ended up scuffling on the floor and was hit on the back of his head, with a bottle.

A few lads joined in, and then scampered away. I asked if he'd seen who bottled him, and is answer was yes, "the big black guy, we had let back in." I had heard enough, this regular had always behaved properly, and certainly had no reason to lie.

I gave Reuben the run down and back in the bar we went. We approached the big guy and told him to leave, his response was "oh no, come on" he wasn't given the chance to say any more, and was taken through the door. A bloke of that size, needing a bottle, what a coward, I thought. The regular had watched us take him out, so I new retribution was close at hand.

After the bar closed, we later found out, the regular and a couple of his friends, had followed the big guy up Broad St. Unsurprisingly, retribution was handed out; and a serious beating followed.

DANGEROUS SITUATIONS

Nobody likes facing situations of danger; a man with a cosh, bottle, or glass, can be quite intimidating. It was another evening at the Pit Stop. Punters indulged in the special offer drinks, so as can be expected; there was a lot of drunkenness. The door staff, was doing the run of the mill things, such as; checking toilets and internal patrols.

It was about nine o'clock and one of the bar staff approached me, looking very worried indeed. "What's wrong with you" I said "a lads smashing bottles against the wall", was his shaky reply.

I asked where he was, then acted accordingly.

Before I even got to the scene, I thought, smashing glass; what an head case. Not only that,but a dangerous head case; I must tread carefully.

Any way, there he was, standing in the middle of the pub; with the look of the Devil. I watched him very closely, before I approached him. I spotted a broken bottle, being held in his right hand.

A sight such as this, really sickens me. Imagine all the decent people, getting themselves ready for a good night out, going to a pub; and encountering someone like this. The very unfortunate, may find they are the subject of a viscous attack; or a broken bottle in the face.

It was time to act. As I approached him, I saw the bottle drop to the floor. The part of his brain that wasn't drunk, was trying to hide the evidence. These kind of people are evil and really make me sick, "you've, been smashing glasses, I want you out". I said,

"Not me mate, not me", was his sorry reply. I had already seen enough, what I was giving him, was the opportunity, to walk out. Most of the time, if you give someone the avenue to retreat, they take it. He stood there, like a drug induced statue, his opportunity to walk, rapidly going.

He stared at me, with bad intention. I was in no mood at all, to wait for the obvious abuse and dealt with him immediately. If a blokes willing to smash glass against a wall and act aggressively, then he must be dealt with. He often needs to be dealt with, in a manner; where the idea to go even further, is totally dispelled.

I held him in a lock, isolating the use of his arms and with the assistance of another doorman, ushered him out. The lad was told to disappear and not to come back again. He stood outside, being verbally abusive; along with his brother, a David Beckham look alike.

Part of me, wanted to run at them, and unleash my anger, but thank God, common sense prevailed. At times like these, a doorman's patience, is truly tested. You stand there being insulted, knowing that in different circumstances, you wouldn't accept it. In the realm of the door however, you must keep your cool.

More often than not, a doorman won't react to the goading. Many have seen it all before and know if they react, the punter will run to the police. If this is the case, a whole new can of worms is released.

Some two months after this incident, the same individual, was thrown out again. I wasn't working that night, but apparently he had started playing up, in the company of his Dad. He obviously thought, being with his father, gave him a licence to misbehave, how wrong he was.

There are some situations which arise, where the opportunity, to get assistance,isn't available. When this happens, you can only rely on your skills, experience and Gods grace.

The area between the toilet, and the bar in the Pit Stop, was notorious for trouble. All the lads would congregate here, and if you were working that area alone, believe you me, it felt alone. I was asked to stand in this area, as lads were starting to get rowdy; and basically do, what drunkard lads do. I stood there, observing the boisterous crowds by the exit door. This particular exit spot, was the only one, that allowed you some sort of OK viewpoint.

I stood there, looking and observing as best I could. I was continually knocking back, the offers of a dance and a free pint; from the over friendly regulars.

Unknown to me at the time, Reuben was doing a toilet check, and in the Pit Stop, this was a very risky affair. I will try explain why and paint a clearer picture of the Pit Stop, through a doorman's eye.

There were never more than three doormen,working at any given time. The door team, literally monitored three hundred plus punters, who regularly came through the door. Bearing this in mind, if you did a toilet check and encountered a problem, you were well and truly on your own. It was practically impossible, to be spotted through the crowd and without the aid of a radio, you were well and truly on your own.

Any way, I was standing at the exit door, when I noticed a punter staring at me. There was no detection of animosity, so I assumed he must have recognised me. The lad then started looking to is left and subtly gesturing. I quickly realised, he was tipping me off and without making it obvious, there was trouble at hand.

I started running through the crowd and as I got closer, I noticed Reuben holding one lad and being confronted, by four more. I could see the anger in their faces and the possibility of a glass, or bottle being used.

The lad being held, was protesting his innocence; as they always do. This however, was no time, for a tit for tat debate. Reuben was well upset and wasted no time in dragging him outside; the lads head, colliding with the door as he did. The rest of his party, were right behind us. I made sure to keep an eye out for any bravery, or a potential sneaky punch.

Reuben was fuming, but managed to calm himself down. I asked him what had happened and he went on to say; I was walking through the crowd and politely said to a guy, "excuse me please", this was met with a mouthful of dismissive profanity. He had considered getting assistance, but the chances were, the lad would of disappeared.

The guy in question, would also prove, very hard to recognise again; especially in such a large crowd. Reuben went onto say, after being spoken to like that, I wasn't going to take the chance, of losing him.

It wasn't just the reply that upset him, but the way in which, he was confronted; by the rest of the group. Reuben felt surrounded and when he was touched, the survival instinct took over.

At the end of the day, everything worked out well. The lad was ejected for his cockiness and Reuben went away unscathed.

As I mentioned before, when this is the outcome, always give God thanks.

The days of the fair go, or one on one, are rapidly disappearing. We are now faced with groups of lads, who together are brave and when intoxicated, braver. Very rarely, are there enough doormen, to deal with a major situation. The masses of punters, far out way, the working door team. What separates the average doormen, is the ability to deal with a situation, with the tools at his disposal. Namely, a sober mind, experience, support of their team, wisdom and lastly, courage.

COMPLACENCY KILLS

Complacency can be a killer. When we get use to our surroundings, it is natural to switch off and take things easy. We instinctively embrace the comfort zone, relax and allow that original edge to waver.

In my opinion, the reason is simply this; we feel very comfortable. We see no need whatsoever, to feel uncomfortable; as far as we are concerned, everyone's my friend. No one would dare upset me, no way. The cleaning phase as been dealt with, the original bad crowd as gone, from here on in, its easy street.

I find, when you've worked the same door, for a considerable length of time,you switch off. Nothing different ever happens, so you lower your guard. You can often allow yourself, to be be lulled into a false sense of security.

Whenever a doorman, is moved to a venue, where he or she, is not accustomed to; he or she, focuses on all around them. They make sure their wits are about them and extremely fine tuned.

The door staff, are preparing themselves for the unknown and taking on a mind set; that is geared around response and reaction. They have come out the comfort zone and their environment, as now become, one of exploration and unease.

This is a natural way to feel, I liken these situations, to the old fashioned spaghetti westerns. The stranger walks into the bar and looks around. The piano stops, everyone looks towards the stranger and inwardly asks the question, who are you then? The stranger then goes to the bar, orders a drink and the piano starts again.

The time between swinging saloon doors, to ordering a drink, is the uncomfortable zone. This is the, I don't know you, you don't know me scenario, but you know the job, I'm here to do. Without a word being spoken, the questions is loud and clear; are you going to make it difficult, or make it easy. What am I up against ?

The unknown, often manifests itself as fear, as we know, fear is a feeling; which can keep us both focused and sharp. It is often when the element of fear goes and is replaced by over confidence, that mistakes happen.

A situation like this, nearly occurred one Thursday night at the Pit Stop. I had been there nearly seven months, so the regulars were familiar with me and me with them. The majority of the lads who came through the door, were normally well behaved and would always shake your hand. The bar, was well known for the young ladies that went there, so consequently, lads would flood through the door.

There was a particular group of lads, who always came, and to be fair, they never really gave us a problem. I never take things for granted and when beer and whiskey is £1 a shot, you never can.

I had sensed a change in the atmosphere, some weeks before and could see trouble surfacing. It had become quite clear, a lot of the original regulars, were no longer coming; and a new crowd, was taking their place.

The bar was packed, as it always was and I remember seeing a lad, roughly six foot three, playing tonsil tennis with a young lady. They were certainly making the most, of the £2 admission fee. I carried on observing the crowd, but nothing out the ordinary was happening. The time was approaching ten thirty pm, with half an hour of my shift left, my mind was starting to wander; the thought of a relaxing wine, was well to the fore.

The young lady, who was previously playing tonsil tennis, suddenly stormed outside. The lady began shouting at Reuben. "Where's the first aid kit, you're all a waste of time, you haven't done nothing",and so on. Reuben looked bewildered, wandering, what on earth is she on about. She was told to calm down and explain herself. She arrogantly declined his offer and stomped off, back to the bar. I watched, as she grabbed the lad she was kissing and shouted to the door-staff "look at his head". I looked at the lad and his head was dripping blood. She pulled him outside and with a mouth full of profanities, disappeared.

Apparently, someone had thrown a glass, which had struck him on the head; thus causing the injuries. Who it was, he didn't say, what he looked like, he didn't know and from the little I'd gathered from Reuben; he seemed very reluctant, to saying anything at all.

My first thoughts were, how could a six foot plus man, get it with a glass and not want to do anything about it. Further more, be happy to leave is Mrs to do all the talking; something just didn't add up. We all stood talking to each other "he should of said something, if were not told, then we cant act, simple".

A few minutes later, a stocky lad called Danny,charged out the bar, looking very upset in deed. I went for a long shot, "were you responsible for that blokes head"? I said, "nothing to do with me boss, it's my cousin I've got a problem with, the little idiot" From having a mystery glass-er in the pub, we've now moved on, to the settling of a family feud.

Danny was part of a group of lads, who came every Thursday and up till now, they had never given us any problems. I knew, that was all about to change.

I asked him what the problem was, and he told me his cousin and his cousins best friend, were threatening him. I told him to relax, "family shouldn't be fighting each other Danny, just ignore him, ignore him", he reluctantly agreed. From enjoying an evening of relative peace and calm, the night was now turning very nasty, to say the least. I finished my counseling session with Danny and left him outside, pondering his next move. Choose wisely Danny, I thought,choose wisely.

I got called to the toilets; lads were urinating every where and trying to open doors, that were meant to be closed. My boss Pete, was doing involuntary overtime, telling lads to sort themselves out and behave. I made sure he was OK and then went back in the bar.

I looked around. How had the pub got into this kind of state, it was truly shocking. I couldn't help but notice, Danny and his cousin, having another heated conversation. Danny had said, they were in the army together, but his cousins mate, was a troublemaker. I waited for a while, then went back to check the toilets. I left the toilet area, satisfied all was well in that department. One less problem to worry about. I re-entered the bar, I could see Danny's pals, but where was Danny. I looked to my left, then looked to my right, bulls eye, there he was.

Danny was charging through the crowd, like the late Jonah Lomu. Beer was splashing everywhere and the punters, were becoming increasingly hostile. They certainly didn't appreciate, his clumsy jinking runs. I ran behind him and used his own momentum, to take him through the door. That was the end of that. The last thing I wanted, was a Rambo impersonator on the loose, especially in the Pit Stop. It was nearly eleven o'clock, so the drinking was effectively over, so he waited outside.

"Anything off the premises is your concern Danny, but you're not coming back in." I left it at that. Danny said, his cousins' pal, had offered him out for a fight, so he was going to sort it out, once and for all. Danny promised, he wouldn't start any trouble in the pub.

Pete called me, with another doormen and pointed to a group of lads, "there all banned," he said. There were about fifteen of them, many of them Danny's pals. "These are all banned, remember the faces, none of them are getting back in." It dawned on me, we could have had a war on our hands, and it would have been messy. Danny had never been a problem before, which was probably why, our attention was never drawn to the group.

What this event clearly brought home was, the bar was heading in the wrong direction. A wake up call was being sent, loud and clear, so we listened. There is a passage in the Bible, which sums this up perfectly, it reads.

1st Thessalonians 5 verse 3

"When they say peace and safety, sudden destruction comes upon them"

PHYSICALLY FIT, DON'T GET HIT

If you're a seven foot giant, with the appearance of hell, the need to get fit, is not a pressing issue. When you're of average build however, i.e. six foot one and twelve stone seven, like me, the need to be physically fit, is very important.

The average street fight, normally finishes in less than sixty seconds. A well aimed punch, on a suspect chin, is normally all that's needed. What happens however, if you're in situation, where you're getting physically tested. The person you're at enmity with, as a reputation, for all out brawling and endurance ? Not only that, if things get violent, the person you're at logger heads with, is not likely to tire.

Having a decent level of fitness, eliminates the worry of tiring, or blowing up. If you end up prematurely tiring, this would often mean defeat. If two men meet, who are equally matched, the deciding factor, is more often than not, fitness. Unless one party, as a far superior fighting technique, then the deciding factor, is nearly always endurance.

The way society as progressed, the one against one, as become something of a rarity. The so called fair fight, as been replaced, with lads jumping individuals, in groups. Nowadays, It would certainly appear, the only fair fights; are in the confines of a boxing ring. Or of course, a well organised, undercover fighting event.

Seeing a punter, go head to head with a doorman, is not really a common site. In certain car parks, on a Friday or Saturday night however, it does happen. The vast majority of doormen I talk to, do some form of training, be it circuit sessions, weight training, or self defence.

A doorman, should never forget who, or what is out there. There are plenty of violent people, who enjoy nothing more,than upsetting the gravy train. When you're on the front line of a door, you have to deal with, boxers, brawlers, rugby players and general street fighters, so you can't take anything for granted.

Bearing all this in mind, and the fact some people possess a Chris Eubank chin, the importance of obtaining a decent level of fitness, is very important. Many great fighters have lost, but no great fighter, as ever become great; without embracing some degree of training.

I have a very god friend, who works the city centre doors; three times world karate champion, Paul Richards. A lot of his students, are doormen; or lads who run their own door firm. Through training at the same gym, we often get to talk about the local city centre problems. It's no secret that violence is on the increase, and punters won't think twice about ;sticking a bottle, or a glass in your face. Due to this state of play, we always end up talking about the same things, i.e. the pubs and clubs at war, where the next riot will be, and who got assaulted at the week end.

One particular area, which we always agree on, is that of personal fitness. Anything that gives you an advantage, is only going to benefit your person. In the job you're doing, that can make all the difference.

Most people, would imagine a world champion to be arrogant, cocky and full of them self. I can sincerely say, after many years of friendship, Paul Richards, is one of the most humble and approachable men I know.

When a man, who is extremely fit and respected, feels the need to maintain is routine, then take heed. The lads within his classes, who are a tough bunch themselves, also feel the need to train; so I think, there's nothing more to say. With the threat of violence a serious issue, one can never feel too sure of themselves.

I remember going to the Lloyds bar on Broad St, with a few friends. We all got to the front door,and stopped. The doorway was blocked, with shouting angry punters, so we decide to hang back and wait. It was clear to all and sundry, that trouble was brewing. I remained alert and made sure, I had my wits about me. The last thing I wanted to do, was walk into a punch, or someone elses cross fire.

The doorway was taken up, with a chubby bloke; with blood pouring from his nose. It didn't take a degree, to guess what had happened. Standing outside on the pavement, was a stocky bloke, with a greying goatee beard; the look of war, etched on his face.

He was certainly no spring chicken, so I quickly assumed, he was either in serious trouble, or just about to get some.

My first impression was, he must be responsible for the bloody nose guy, standing in the doorway. The manner in which he stared towards the door, seemed to confirm it. I expected a continuation, of whatever had started and everyone stood and watched.

Different punters were leaving the bar, and walking straight past him; then one particular bloke stopped. No one had any idea, as to what was going to happen next. I watched as the bloke walked straight towards him, then within a split second, 'bang!' he produced a headbutt, The goatee beard chap, was knocked-out. A couple of lads, helped goatee to his unsteady feet; and he fell into the arms of a sobbing girlfriend.

The doormen cleared the entrance and everyone carried on into the bar. I thought to myself WOW. People just laughed and joked, as though nothing serious had happened. We live in a very violent, and dangerous world people. My prayer to everyone reading my book is, never forget it.

BOTTLE IS A SCIENCE

oday's life style, can be very hectic. Our bodies respond to what we call, the fight or flight syndrome. In times of fear and stress,our bodies, produce enough adrenaline; to fight the problems we face. Or consequently, give you enough adrenalin, to run to safety.

When faced with threatening situations, mankind, still resorts to a primitive escape mechanism. This mechanism is referred to as, the fight or flight syndrome.

I read a brief article, which drew the example of prehistoric man, facing a saber tooth tiger. In prehistoric times, the cave-dweller, would go out to hunt and would often be the hunted. As we know from the history books, beasts were very big and very dangerous. When the cave dweller, was faced by the tiger, adrenaline would be released into his system. If the situation called for attack, the adrenaline would be utilised, for attack. If the situation called for flight, the adrenaline would be utilised, for flight.

Our bodies react to stress, in a similar way they react to fear. We experience fear, when we have cause to be concerned; about our safety. We experience stress, when we are in situations, where we feel under threat; but are not actually in any immediate danger.

When we feel under threat in this way, our bodies respond, with the fight or flight syndrome. This syndrome, which prepares our bodies to fight or flee, involves a number of physical changes. Our heart-rate increases, our breathing becomes shallow and all of our senses work better. We may have a desire to defecate, our muscles tense to fight or flee. Our hands and feet begin to sweat, to cool ourselves. All of these changes, make us hot.

The fight or flight syndrome, is our instinctive reaction to danger. This response however, can be set off by many situations, that are not really dangerous, or life threatening. But our bodies, are reacting as if our lives, were actually being threatened. The reaction to such a threat, is a powerful one. When there is no enemy to fight or run from, the physical feelings created by the fight or flight syndrome, have no release; and so we begin to build up stress. When we examine the bodily reaction to fear, we quickly realise, its nothing new, examples are;

PRE- FIGHT SHAKES

Arms and legs start to tremble and you feel out of control.

PERSPIRATION

Hands and forehead start to sweat, if you've got money on a horse; in a photo finish, you'll understand.

DRY MOUTH AND SHAKY VOICE

Your mouth becomes dry and when you speak, your words are jumbled and are delivered shakily.

BUTTERFLIES IN GUT

Constant desire to want the toilet.

YELLOW FEVER

This is where, the adrenalin released, plays havoc with your body. Quite frankly, the lack of control, as brought about a feeling of despair. Helplessness and shear terror, often follow.

All of these feelings, are quite natural and part of the bodily chemistry of adrenalin. When you can ignore them and deal with them in a positive way, then the negative feelings, that often accompany them, start to take a back seat.

We need to remember, under perceived threatening conditions, mankind still resorts to a primitive escape mechanism. Our heart beats faster, adrenalin races through are system, blood pressure rises, breathing speeds up and are muscles begin to tense. This bodily reaction, is preparing us emotionally, for confrontation and for early man, it was a daily experience.

If we were to examine our lives and the violent scenarios we've faced, we would find many examples; of the fight or flight scenario. The meeting of two rival gangs, is one example; with one charging and the other running. Though this can be looked on, as a collective fleeing, for the individual, it represents a personal decision. Another example, is the challenging of the pub bully and watching them visibly shake. They noticeably grow smaller, by the second. How often, were you in a situation, where someone talked a very good fight. They portrayed themselves as a rock and when you confronted them, they fled down the road?

An example, could be that of our own Frank Bruno. When Frank fought Tyson, in their first boxing encounter, his attitude and approach were there for all to see. Although he got floored, he almost instantly got up and stared at Tyson. Franks expression,was one of real bad intent. Tyson said himself, when he looked at Frank, he could tell he came to fight. Frank went on to shake up Tyson, with a serious left hook and if a sustained attack was carried out, he may well have knocked him out. He entered the ring, knowing he was going to war; with the most feared boxer of his era. Frank dealt with his nerves and emotions admirably. Though he went on to lose, you couldn't fault his bravery and certainly not his attitude.

When we look at Bruno v Tyson II, we see a totally different Frank. It was clear to all observers, in fight I, he was extremely focused and in control of his emotions. Fight II however, reflected a boxer, who looked less than confident. Unlike fight I, where Frank got caught early and came back fighting, his response in fight II, was the total opposite. Franks fighting instincts, seemed to cave in and within that first exchange; the result became clear. Tyson went on to overwhelm Frank and for all the fans watching, the result became a formality.

I must make it perfectly clear. Frank Bruno deserves the world of respect. Any man who uses their God given talents, too earn a fortune, as nothing to prove. Frank is an example to all of us; of just what can be accomplished,if only we try.

PROFESSIONAL PEACE-MAKER

I find this, the most important and rewarding aspect of the job. The role of the peace maker. Praise God.

Without doubt, the vast majority of doormen, can stop fights. The hard part however, is stopping the fight, before it starts; by the implementation of, verbal diffusion.

There are plenty rough, tough and strong doormen around, who can always be relied upon, for physical support. I'm quite sure, these particular individuals, wouldn't let you down.

Unfortunately, the same can't be said, for those who have the skill and ability, to diffuse a potential altercation. The goal of the doormen, is to intervene verbally and subdue any trouble, without the physical being applied.

Bouncers are a funny breed. The term bouncer, presents an image of someone who will break up fights and forcibly eject, obnoxious punters from the premises.

Bouncers, are often portrayed in movies, as rough, tough, thug like scrappers. They love to fight and bruise, like in the movie Road House.

Many night clubs, foster that image. They make a point, of hiring intimidating hulks, or seven foot giants. Doormen like these however, are sometimes unfairly judged.

I genuinely believe, some places need that sort of muscle. Some bars are battle zones and to be honest, only a certain type of bouncer, can deal with it. In many cases, only the tough doormen, get any respect, from the local tough guys. I am a realist and there are some situations, or lets say bars, where horses for courses spring to mind.

Usually, the big bruiser type bouncers, have little experience, in dealing with verbal issues. Oftentimes, this isn't their fault, as they haven't received any verbal coaching, or any real training. In a crisis, these enormous bouncers, will be forced to rely on their own instincts and ideas. When you're built like a man mountain, the results can often be devastating.

I don't want to come across, like all big doormen, are lacking in verbal skills. The fact is however, if you're twenty stone and six foot eight, most punters wont question a request. Or try and create a situation, where your physical prowess, is going to be tested.

So on the rare occasion, when it does happen, it often,brings about a reaction; which is instinctive, rather than practiced. i.e.

a punch to the chin, for the disrespectful challenge; as apposed to to a dismissive sentence.

The first reaction, will result in the punter being punched.

The second reaction, will leave the punter with his teeth intact; and no one knocking your door.

The duty of a bouncer, is to monitor the crowd, to see that everyone behaves; the goal should be, everyone has a good time. All within the boundaries of the club,of course.

The best bouncers, are often personable, friendly and can talk to people; without appearing threatening, or intimidating. The best bouncers, are the ones who avoid, having to bounce anyone. They talk to people, with due respect shown to them. They speak in a way, where their authority isn't questioned or doubted. The mere presence of a well trained bouncer, will remind the punter, their conduct is being scrutinised. If the punter goes too far, action is inevitable.

No one likes being bumped into. Whether a bus queue, concert hall, street corner, or supermarket. Wherever it may be, no none likes being bumped into, period.

In a crowded pub or party, you simply can't avoid being knocked about. Your patience often becomes severely tested, especially if an expected apology isn't forth coming. If the bumping continues to happen, you often feel the need to react and make your feelings known, to the guilty party.

Try and imagine yourself in a pub environment and being continually buffeted about. On top of all this, you've been drinking continuously. You're trying your best to suppress the growing anger inside, but one more nudge and you know the outcome. This is where, you're entering into the world, of the angry punter.

The chances are, you're a very decent person, but alcohol; can make a persons character, dramatically change.

In the over crowded pub scenario, you always get an argument, stemming from an accidental shove. This can easily result, in an unwanted punch up. Some situations,can be spotted straight away. You see two faces staring at each other, evil glances are exchanged and violent intentions manifest.

This is a situation, where verbal skills, can diffuse a potential battle. If you're dealing with two decent enough people, the result is often a peaceful one. If I see a situation like this occurring, I react immediately and my approach often goes like this.

"Is every thing alright lads"? This would be met with the problem. In this scenario, were dealing with the accidental shove, causing beer to spill. Straight away, my presence there, as sent a message and the message is clear. You've been spotted lads and if it goes any further, the team will act.

I would never tell a person, who as spilled someone's drink, to buy them one back. The sole purpose of me being there, is to quench the flames, not to add fuel to the fire. Personally, an order such as 'buy one back' is over stepping my authority and the person in question, may not have the money to do so.

My suggestion, could cause them embarrassment; especially if they feel, put on the spot. I would proceed with.

"You seem like decent lads, who have come for a good night out" Even if, deep down, they look like trouble, at least your making them feel like they're not, "don't let one shove spoil the night lads", I would tell the lad who feels hard done by "the pubs packed mate, its hard not to get bumped into" followed by, "come on lads I'm sure it was an accident". The response I receive,would give me a clear indication, of where were at. It would also determine, whether or not the problem is going to be forgotten, or taken any further; normally, common sense would prevail.

I don't want to insult any one, by pretending things are always that easy. I am just trying to put across an approach, that as often worked for me. This approach, was successfully used in a bar, that attracted hundreds of punters. We sold beer and spirits, at one pound a drink; with only the three doormen to keep the peace.

We need to remember, the majority of punters are good people and if you give them the opportunity to see sense, they often take it. If a potential battle, is solved with a handshake, or the buying of a drink, then praise God. You're a professional peace maker and when peace is the end result, you've done your job.

Through displaying verbal skills and not charging in like an elephant, you can save yourself a world of trouble; and who knows, your actions may even save a life.

'Save a life'? Too many, that may seem far fetched, or totally over the top, 'save a punters life Elvis, you're having a laugh mate.

How many cases have there been, where someone's lost their life, to a single punch? Or a single kick to the head? The answer is plenty. All it takes, is one well aimed blow, striking the right spot. Violence can be deadly and in the blink of an eye, you can have a fatality on your hands.

Sometimes, I might look at things a little deeper than most. When you've seen certain things happen in front of you, its easy to focus on the worse scenarios. "Why" ? you might ask. The answer is a simple one. I've seen the worse scenarios.

When you've seen a lot of bad things and been part of it, you start to desire something better. That in my opinion, is always a peaceful outcome.

Sometimes I stand by the D.J consul and watch all the punters dancing away. I see them laughing, joking and generally enjoying themselves. I smile to myself and think, that's how it should be. I look at the young drinkers, who have just turned eighteen and acting like they've been partying for years. The truth is however, if they never had their passports handy, they would have be refused entry and sent on their way.

What really hits home however, is the realisation, that the punters need us. A lot of them don't know it, and wont admit it, but believe you me, they need us.

Many young punters, are just starting to learn about life and the social arena of adulthood. They think they know it all and lets be honest, so did we, when we were teenagers.

The difference is however, if we got lippy, we would get a clip round the ear hole. Nowadays however, if you get to lippy, there's every chance, you'll get kicked from pillar to post. The bullies and trouble makers that lurk around the bars, have no mercy; and they always look for easy targets to threaten. Our very presence, be it on the front door, or walking through the lounge of a pub, can make all the difference. Seeing a figure of authority, often dissuades, any potential trouble maker,from starting trouble. The fact were willing to protect the defenseless, and allow the people of the town, to enjoy themselves; shouldn't be underestimated. If we allow people the opportunity, to enjoy themselves; without fear of attack,then that's a thumbs up. It also places us, ladies and gentlemen, in the realm of the professional peace maker. After all folks, that's what were being paid to do.

I remember working at a hard core rave, in a warehouse in Bordesley Green,which is in Birmingham. This was your typical venue, cold, dark and very loud.

The conditions, were the last thing on peoples mind, as this particular warehouse, was jam-packed to the rafters. Inside the warehouse, were many rooms. There was the main dance area, which was enormous, linked together with two other rooms; which for want of a better description, I'll call black holes.

The crowd was rocking to the beats in the main area, while the pitch black chill out rooms, were being used for anything and everything.

I watched as the crowds rocked to the underground acid and I noticed a bloke, who seemed more than a little merry. I followed him around, praying he didn't fall down a hole, or put his foot through the main speaker box.

I was finding it quite amusing, watching him turn left, right and then left again. What he did next however, was far from amusing. I watched like a guardian angel; as my drunkard friend, headed for the chill out room and I could just make out, his hands rubbing against the walls. What's he up to? I thought.

The Lone Ranger, as I will refer to him, got tired of wandering around in darkness, so focused is senses on the electrical system.

I entered the chill out room, not really knowing what to expect, and boom, the lights came on. Everyone covered their eyes in shock. It was an apostle Paul, experience. Read your Bibles, Acts chapter 9.

The Lone Ranger, had found the light switch; how he did it, I'll never know. Five minutes earlier, he could hardly put one foot in front of another, but somehow, he found the light switch. All heads turned to Ranger, the promoter wanted blood and he wanted it now.

Ranger was punched by the promoter and his pal and dragged out the chill out room, to an outside yard. I knew he was moments away from a severe beating, or possibly worse, so I stayed close by. I followed them to the yard, and before another right hook was landed, I intervened. I grabbed hold of Ranger and told the promoter, I would deal with it. The promoter looked at me, as if to say, whats he to you? I repeated myself again "ill deal with it" the promoter stared at me, then walked away.

I looked at Ranger and laughed. There was no way on earth, I was going to let him get beaten up. The man was drunk and probably didn't even know where he was. "Consider it your lucky day mate". "you walked into the lions den, put your head in its mouth and will live to tell the tale". I said.

Moments like these, can be quite refreshing. At the end of the day, I had nothing to prove, so why hospitalise the guy. It's nice to know, kindness and compassion, still exists. From being moments away from blood guts and possible death, Ranger was safe. I pointed him towards the taxi rank and watched him meander off.

Every man is guilty of all the good he didn't do,
Voltaire (Francois Marie Arouet)

It was my night off, so I decided to go to the pit stop for a couple of drinks, with the boss Pete. I said my hello's to Reuben and Kevin, who were working the door, then headed to the bar. The fact I was driving, kept any drinking to a minimum, so being sober, I noticed everything around me. The bar was closing, so the punters reluctantly made their way to the exits; with the exception of a couple of lads, who were drinking at zero m-p-h.

One lad in particular, had been told to drink up, on several occasions; and his response was far from friendly. I watched as Kevin engaged in a heated conversation and knew what was coming next. Reuben took the lad in a head lock and ushered him through the door, his mate soon followed.

With the excitement over, I finished off my drink and got ready to disappear. The bar staff was sitting down; enjoying a well earned drink and basically switched off for the night. I got off my stool, stretched my bones, as you do, and then looked towards the door. The two chaps, who had been thrown out, were staring into the pub, and one lad in particular, looked ready for a fight.

Reuben got up and headed for the exit door, Kevin and I followed him. The lad who had been head locked, pointed at Reuben and said "I wanted a good look at your face, I'll be back" Reubens reply was "you're here now, so what's stopping you"?

The closer Reuben got to him, the further away the lad stepped, and at one point, he looked on the brink of running. I could tell by the look on his face, that he wasn't up for any fighting. This was nothing more than a simple case of bravado. The lad hurriedly made his way up the stairs and shouted down "watch your back"

I could foresee a bloody outcome, so I stepped up my pace and called him to stop. The bloke was looking for respect, but the way he was talking, he was heading for a punch. He was aggrieved at being held in a headlock, and told me it was bang out of order. At this point, his mate aired his views, but made it known, he didn't want any trouble. I put the situation to them in simple terms, "you're unhappy about the headlock, but that's happened and it can't be changed". I went onto say "coming back to the pub, and making threats, leaves the situation open".I pointed out to the chap "this means you're a danger ".

I was letting him know, exactly how it stood; at no point did I raise my voice, or act aggressively. I told them, what's done is done, and if you never resorted to swearing and aggression, we wouldn't be here now.

The lads started name dropping and mentioning certain tough individuals, they were supposedly connected to. I knew straight away, this was their last show of strength and a desperate attempt, at gaining some sort of respect.

I smiled to myself and asked them, if they wanted me to phone one of the names ? I pointed out to them, the names are all in my phone. I smiled at their response and the way their expressions changed. For them, their ace card, had been totally torn apart.

I gave them the opportunity to end it with a little bit of pride intact and if they chose wisely, it would be over. If not however, they could never say, the chance wasn't there.

Thankfully, the situation was ended peacefully, with apologies, smiles and hand shakes being offered. This was the outcome I had wanted and when things fall into place, it's always a nice feeling.

MY GREATEST DECISION

The greatest ten metre walk,I've ever made, was when I walked from the back of my local church,to the front. This happened on New Years Eve 2017. I asked Jesus Christ to come into my life and I have never looked back since. To all my friends out there, you are continually in my prayers and placed before God. If you're reading this book, know one thing, God is good and worthy to be praised. If you have a spare few minutes, look at YouTube, "Charles Lawson,Death then judgment". Take care everyone and bless.

RESPECT TO THE BOYS

This goes out to all my friends, who shared in the ups and downs of my life, big respect. If I fail to mention anyone, then you have my sincere apologies.

The original Saltley boys;
Caines, Patrick, Batson, Wayne aka Bass, Max, Howard, Peter aka Shirley, Eddy and Clive

As time passed, we grew from being a relatively small number of lads, to a large group. This brought about the inclusion of some proper good chaps. Big Bird, Sean, Dean, Bosley, Giles, Prof, Shamus and the late Big T. You have all played a large part in my life, and you will continually be in my prayers.

SUMMARY

Though I don't like to admit it, I am not getting any younger. The risks I took, as a younger reckless man, are very much memories. There are some that make me cringe and shake my head, and many more, that make me smile and laugh. The door game as been an interesting adventure. Now I see it for what it is, a risky Job, that can lead to disfigurement, prison, friendships, love and pain. For many the door game is a way of earning extra income, with the added bonus of loyal friends at your side. The door game as thrown up many acquaintances; whether they'll turnout to be life long friends, remains to be seen.

One thing I've learned however, is this. The door game, is just another job, only a lot more dangerous and at times unrewarding.

The older you get, the more you honour the things in life, that will bring you sincere happiness. Family, friends, and a content life. Stay safe people, God is good. Bless.

Trevor Alton Smith aka "Big T"

I knew Trevor, for well over thirty five years. We both went to Hodge Hill Comprehensive School, in Birmingham. Trevor was also the uncle to my two daughters, Alana and Christina. Big Trevor,was sadly shot, by a police marksman and is truly missed, by both friends and family.

Gary Twist

March 63 – Oct 2017

Both Gary and myself, went to Hodge Hill School. We also worked together as doormen, at Bonds Nightclub. Gary was assaulted and sadly lost his life. Gary Twist, you are missed by all your friends and family.

Paul Burke was a person, who could be both humorous and very serious. I have had many discussions with Paul and always considered him an intelligent person, who tried to enjoy life as best he could. Without a shadow of a doubt, he loved to share a smile and engage in laughter, with those, who were around him.

Mr Paul Antony Burke.

I remember going through a difficult phase of my life, due to health issues. On one of my visits to the local hospital, I bumped into Jel.

We laughed, embraced, then laughed some more. I asked if he was still in touch with many of the old chaps, he smiled broadly and said, "yeah, there still about Elv".

We had a brief discussion about the old days, smiled and embraced for the final time. Not long after this chance meeting, I got the sad news, Jel had passed away. Jel, you are missed by all.

Jernal Singh aka Jel

July 1967-April 2010

Printed in the United States
By Bookmasters